SEASONS, SAINTS & STICKY TAPE

**Ideas and Activities for
Celebrating Christian Festivals**

Nicola Currie and Jean Thomson

Illustrations by Julie Baines

National Society/Church House Publishing
Church House, Great Smith Street, London SW1P 3NZ

ISBN 0 7151 4820 6

First published in 1992 by The National Society (Church of England) for Promoting Religious Education and Church House Publishing

The authors and publisher wish to express their thanks to:

Many diocesan children's advisers for their help and advice.

The authors wish to thank the Church Times for permission to reproduce some material from the fortnightly Allsorts page.

The parish of Banbury and St Paul's Sunday School for their help and support.

Ruth Lewis, Children's Officer, Christian Aid, for her work on the Christian Aid chapter.

The Revd Canon Andrew Bowden, Rector of Coates, Rodmarton, Sapperton with Frampton Mansell, for his suggestions for the family service ideas for a Patronal Festival.

Bible quotations are from *The Jerusalem Bible* (JB), © Darton, Longman and Todd Ltd and Doubleday and Company Inc.; the *Good News Bible* (GNB), © American Bible Society, New York; and *The Revised Standard Version* (RSV), © The Division of Christian Education of the National Council of the Churches of Christ in the USA.

Darton, Longman & Todd for an extract from *In Search of Julian of Norwich* by Sheila Upjohn; HarperCollins for a prayer from *The Cloud of Witnesses*; and The O'Brien Press for an extract from *The Real Story of Patrick* by George Otto Simms.

Material from *The Alternative Service Book 1980* is reproduced by permission of The Central Board of Finance of the Church of England.

We are grateful to the following for permission to reproduce photographs:

Ateliers et Presses de Taizé, page 66; Bridgeman Art Library, London, page 15; Dave Clark, Folly Trust, pages 34, 84; Christian Aid, pages 48, 50, 51; Ecumenical Society of the Blessed Virgin Mary, page 12; Euredition bv, The Hague, page 9; Jane Gray, page 22; The Julian Shrine, Norwich, page 44; Virginia Merrill, The Episcopal News, page 74; Bernard Merry, page 81; The Trustees of The National Gallery, London, page 37; Northern Ireland Tourist Board, page 28; One World Week, page 70; David Silverberg, p. 31; St David's Cathedral, Dyfed, page 25; RJL Smith, Much Wenlock, page 59; Verlag Aurel Bongers, Recklinghausen, pages 18, 52, 55; Woodmansterne (Jeremy Marks), pages 40, 78.

Illustrations by Julie Baines
Cartoons by Taffy Davies
Cover photograph by Dave Clark, Folly Trust
Cover design by Leigh Hurlock
Text design by Andy Haughton, aj designs
Printed in England by Orphans Press

CONTENTS

INTRODUCTION

Seasons, Saints & Sticky Tape is a practical resource book on Christian festivals and saints' days. It is a book for all who work with children under eleven in church groups, schools, midweek clubs, family services and those one-off special occasions.

There are 24 chapters which provide ideas for celebrating the Christian faith throughout the year. They are loosely based on the Church of England calendar of saints' days and festivals. Two other celebrations, Christian Aid Week and One World Week, are also included.

The action-packed chapters give background historical information, biblical starting points, discussion questions, all-age worship ideas and suggestions for practical activities. The emphasis is on learning through experience and many of the suggestions are for events or craft activities. Varied and full of fun they range from a Mexican *Posada* party for Advent to a hose trumpet for St Cecilia's day.

Stories of the saints have inspired and encouraged many people in their faith. The activities in *Seasons, Saints & Sticky Tape* take an aspect of the faith of a saint and relate it to the life experience of a child - a prayer walk for St Aidan, a rule of life for St Francis, and a Celtic cross for St David.

Seasons, Saints & Sticky Tape provides an opportunity for sharing and celebrating together the pilgrimage of faith.

How to use this book:

Seasons, Saints & Sticky Tape is a book to dip into. Some suggestions will need to be adapted to suit your local conditions. Others will need advance planning so that the necessary materials for the activities can be collected before the session. We have assumed that a standard session will last roughly half an hour.

The 1989 Children Act specifies the amount of care and supervision necessary for children, particularly the under eights. If the event you are planning will last over two hours and involves the care of the under eights then you must inform the local authority Social Services department. The Children Act requires you to inform the department in advance and you will need to register with them if your two hour sessions become frequent events.

Advent

The Journey to Bethlehem

Advent marks the beginning of the Christian year. It is a time of penitence, preparation and waiting for the coming (in Latin *adventus*) of Christ at Christmas. For children Advent is a season of great excitement and anticipation of what is to come. Many will be familiar with the Advent wreath or crown and will light a candle on each of the four Sundays of Advent. Some churches link the candles with the Sunday readings. An attractive and effective way to link the traditional readings for Advent, the themes of preparation, concern for others, and spiritual readiness is by adapting the Mexican custom of the *Posada.*

Posada literally means hospitality, inn or place of shelter. It is an old custom probably introduced into Latin America by Spanish friars. The ritual focuses on two of the Gospel themes for the season: the rejection of Joseph and Mary by the innkeepers at Bethlehem (representing the rejection of unpopular demands for righteous living) and the joy at the birth of the Christ child (representing the joy that comes from welcoming and accepting God into our lives).

In Mexico, the *Posada* is a re-enactment by the whole community over a series of nine nights of the drama of the entry into Bethlehem. Each night a group of worshippers gathers at someone's house carrying statues of Joseph, Mary and a donkey. The people sing songs and ask to enter different homes but for the first eight nights they are not welcomed in. On the final night they are welcomed into a home and there is a great celebration with songs and special food.

ACTIVITY IDEAS

Timing

The *Posada* can be telescoped into an afternoon or evening party on the fourth Sunday in Advent. Alternatively each Sunday in Advent can be used to prepare for the *Posada*. The suggestions for Advent 2 and Advent 3 are ideas for the theme only and need to be augmented to suit the local situation.

Advent I - Preparation for the festival

Advent is a time for spiritual and material preparation. The first Sunday can focus on the preparation of the festivities for the final party. In Mexico children receive their gifts in a *piñata* - a brightly coloured clay pot filled with tiny presents and sweets. This is hung up and then broken by the children on Christmas day. Here are two ways you can make a simple *piñata*.

1. Tape together two small shallow plastic bowls (individual Greek yogurt pots or dessert containers are ideal). Wire wool can be used to erase the product design.

2. Separate one unit from a cardboard egg box leaving the hinge in place. Cut down to form a neat shape and cover the outside with small pieces of white paper. Tape together the two halves.

Remember to enclose small wrapped sweets into the *piñatas* before taping the halves together. The *piñatas* can then be decorated with Christmas motifs using paint, colouring materials or sticky paper. Once completed they can be hung up in the party room or on the parish Christmas tree. In Mexico children knock down their *piñatas* from a tree. It might be able to adapt this custom and use the *piñatas* in some Christmas games.

Advent 2 - Concern for the world

By tradition this Sunday is a time to focus on the prophets. The prophets criticised people who worshipped God by their words but not by their lives. They spoke out against those who ignored injustice and wrong-doing. The prophets taught that God would send his Messiah to put things right.

You will need

cardboard egg boxes or shallow container bowls

sticky tape

paper

decorative shapes

glue

gift ribbon

drawing or painting materials

small sweets

Christians believe that Jesus is this Messiah.

In preparation for the *Posada* you can explore the theme of injustice with the children. Just as the innkeepers rejected Mary and Joseph at the first Christmas so today people continue to reject or have no care for the homeless, the poor, the handicapped and the victims of injustice. This Sunday is an appropriate time to consider charities that work to fight injustice, need and poverty in the world.

Advent 3 - Spiritual preparation

John the Baptist is traditionally the focus for the third Sunday in Advent. His message of repentance and preparation for the coming of the Messiah reminds us that we need to prepare spiritually for the coming of Christ at Christmas.

Before the class prepare cards with each letter of the word CHRISTMAS written on a separate card. Ask the children to make each separate letter the initial letter of a word at the beginning of a prayer for Christmas. For example the C of Christmas could become "Care for the old and needy", or "Christ help us prepare for your birthday". These cards can then be fixed on a string and hung in the party room for the *Posada* party.

You will need

cards

hole-punch

string

drawing materials

Advent 4 - the journey to Bethlehem - a Posada

In advance of the Posada you will need to:

* prepare a party room

* prepare materials for a short service (see *The Promise of His Glory: Services and Prayers for the Season from All Saints to Candlemas,* CHP/Mowbray)

* prepare refreshments (if the group wants to prepare authentic Mexican Christmas food the book *Christmas - a Cook's Tour* by Ingeborg Relph and Penny Stanway, Lion, is a useful resource)

* get fancy dress clothes

* have enough copies of carol sheets

* give notice to parishioners you will call on

This Sunday is the time for the *Posada* and party. Here the journey to Bethlehem is re-enacted. Traditionally this is the Sunday when we remember Mary, her longing for God and her patient waiting and preparation for his arrival. Encourage the children to help prepare the party room to welcome Christ at Christmas.

For the *Posada* one child needs to be Mary and another Joseph. You can have a 'donkey' too and the children can dress up as different people. Perhaps they could be people who are often rejected. Alternatively it could be an occasion for dressing up in different national costumes to represent the message of Christmas going out to the world.

The *Posada* needs to be adapted to suit local conditions. Ensure that there is enough adult supervision and that a number of parishioners know that they will be visited. Walk with the children around part of the parish singing carols. At the homes of the chosen parishioners get 'Mary' and 'Joseph' to knock on the door and ask for a room for the night. The parishioners need to act as the belligerent innkeepers who will reject the group. The group finally arrives at the Church where they are welcomed with open arms by the congregation. There can then be a short service or Blessing of the Crib. The joy of Christmas is celebrated and the children are welcomed again in the Christian community. The service is followed by a party.

St Nicholas

A Saint for Everyone

Saint Nicholas. Early nineteenth-century folk icon from the Balkans

St Nicholas is a universally popular saint - a great miracle worker and archetypal superman. Nicholas sorts out the goodies from the baddies and puts the world to rights in the name of God.

Legends about him abound and his patronage includes children, sailors, unmarried girls, merchants, pawnbrokers, apothecaries, perfumiers, little boys, scholars, parish clerks, Aberdeen, New York and Russia. He appears everywhere from Russian icons to Christmas cards. Being an adaptable figure this great Christian saint has become immortalised in our secular culture as Santa Claus.

Very little is known about the life of Nicholas other than that he was a 4th century bishop of Myra (modern Mugla, in south western Turkey). One tradition says that he was imprisoned during the persecution of the Emperor Diocletian. Well-known in the East by the 6th century, his popularity was enhanced by a fictitious biography written by Methodius in the 9th century. This biography recounts many legends about Nicholas, whose holiness is shown by the close affinity of his life to that of Christ. Like Christ he performs miracles, stills storms, cares for the needy, suffers and dies.

The most famous legend about St Nicholas tells how he threw three bags of gold into the room of three daughters of an impoverished nobleman, thus saving them from prostitution. Other versions say that St Nicholas put the money in the girls' stockings at the end of the beds and was chased by the girls' father who wanted to know who the benefactor was. The three stockings are said to be the origin of the pawnbroker's sign of three gold balls. The story may also have given rise to the practice of hanging up stockings at Christmas, to the popularity of chocolate coins and to the custom of putting new coins into stockings.

In many parts of Europe including Germany, Holland and Austria, Saint Nicholas is said to visit the homes of children near his feast day on 6 December. He leaves presents of sweets, fruits and nuts for the children in shoes they have left out for him. Dutch immigrants took their traditions to America and the Dutch St Nicholas, *Sinterklaas*, who was adopted in the New World, eventually became the modern Santa Claus we know today.

ACTIVITY IDEAS

Themes

The legends about St Nicholas provide a wealth of material for children. One way to link the stories about St Nicholas with the traditions of his feast day is to have a children's Christmas party on St Nicholas' Day or the Sunday after.

Timing

The activities suggested here are interrelated and can form a whole afternoon's party activities. Alternatively each activity could take one session.

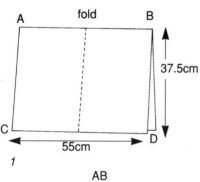

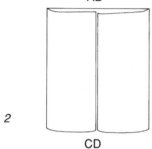

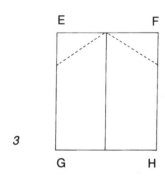

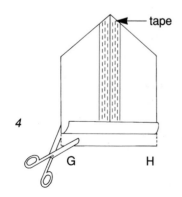

1. Bishops and Mitres

Before the reign of Elizabeth I many English cathedrals and schools observed the custom of a Boy Bishop on St Nicholas' Day. A boy would be chosen from the cathedral or parish choir to become a bishop. He was dressed in boy-sized bishop's vestments and presented with a mitre and crozier. During his term of office he was expected to perform the role of a bishop and preach a sermon. He was also able to award special privileges and treats.

Explain to the children that a bishop is the leader of a spirit-filled community and that a bishop's mitre is meant to remind people of the tongues of fire that seemed to descend upon the Apostles on the first day of Pentecost. Paper mitres can be made and decorated by the children. Once completed these mitres could be put outside the party room and secretly filled with chocolate coins by a 'St Nicholas'. The group might choose a boy or girl bishop to hold office during the party.

1) Take a sheet of paper 75cm x 55cm (the smaller measurement needs to be the circumference of the child's head). Fold the rectangle in half as shown and press down fold. Turn the paper 90° and fold in half again. Unfold.

2) Then fold sides AC and BD to the centre fold as shown.

3) Fold down points E and F to the central fold. Crease and then unfold. Tuck in points E and F along the new crease to produce the point of a mitre.

4) Secure the centre join with tape. Snip with scissors up folds G and H. Gather three sheets at the front of the mitre and fold up. Secure with tape. Turn over and fold up remaining sheet, securing with tape. Decorate the mitre.

2. Alphabet Biscuits

St Nicholas is believed to know the name of every child he visits. In Holland and Germany parents buy an initial letter of their child's name made from chocolate to give to them on St Nicholas' Day. Alphabet biscuits are also common.

The biscuit dough can be made before the session for the children to mould into initial letters during the party. The quantities given here make 20 biscuits.

* Rub the fat into the flour and spices.

* Cream the egg with the sugar and add to the flour and fat mixture to form a soft dough.

* Roll the dough into sausages about 1cm thickness and shape initial letters from them.

* Prick out decorations in the letters.

* Bake at Gas Mark 4/180ºC/350ºF for 15 minutes until golden brown.

You will need

75g butter or margarine

175g plain flour

1 small egg

75g brown sugar

1tsp cinnamon

pinch of cloves and cardamom

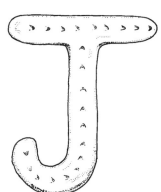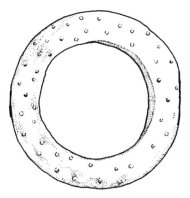

3. Stockings and Coins

Tell the children the story of St Nicholas and the three girls' stockings.

One way to bring the story alive for children is to play a throwing game. Place a cardboard box on a table as the 'window' and let the children throw gold chocolate coins into the box, just as St Nicholas threw coins into the girls' bedroom. Those who succeed can eat their coins.

Another way to enliven the story is to play a chasing game. Ask the children to form a ring and lie on their stomachs with their heads facing the centre. They have to pretend to be asleep. A 'St Nicholas' then has to tiptoe around the outside of the circle and drop a bag of coins at the feet of one of the children. If the child hears the bag drop he has to chase St Nicholas, just as the girls' father chased the saint in the legend. The children can take it in turns to be St Nicholas and at the end of the game they can all share the chocolate coins.

You will need

cardboard box

chocolate gold coins

Christmas

The Arrival of a New-born Baby

The Virgin and Child (from The Ecumenical Society of the Blessed Virgin Mary)

Children need no introduction to Christmas but the familiarity of the Christmas story and its traditions always run the risk of obscuring its real meaning. The real St Nicholas has undergone many changes to become Santa Claus; our giving of gifts carries only the faintest echo of God's giving of his Son. Yet these traditions were originally intended to help explain to children the meaning of the Christmas story.

Today we need reminding of the true significance of Christmas. Children still need to go back to Bethlehem and see the Christ child for themselves. Cribs, nativity plays, carols, and Christingles may be familiar to adults but they are often new and exciting for young children. Here we suggest an approach which supplements the other, readily available, traditional customs by starting to look at the Christmas story from the children's own experience of new birth and babies.

ACTIVITY IDEAS

Themes

Most children are able to identify in some way with the birth of a baby. Getting them to think about a new baby is a useful introduction to help children understand more about Jesus' birth. These activities are designed so that the teacher can first explore the themes common to the Christmas story and the birth of a child - the excitement, the preparation and the response of people to the birth. The children can then choose which activity they want to pursue.

Timing

This material can take one or two sessions.

1. The Excitement of the Pregnancy

Read the annunciation story to the children, Luke 1.26-56.

Mary is overwhelmed with joy at the news of her pregnancy and the gift of her son:"My heart praises the Lord; my soul is glad because of God my Saviour," (GNB). Discuss with the children how they would feel if they were going to have a new brother or sister.

Parents often record the events leading up to the birth of their baby and the birth itself by starting a baby album before the child is born. Get one of the parents of a new-born baby to bring in a baby album to show the children. Ask the children what events they think they might put in an album before a baby is born - a family tree, pictures of the grandparents, a hospital/GP visits card, the home, etc

You will need

a baby album

a Bible

if possible a new mother and baby and a suitcase full of things she might have needed for a new baby

gifts people might give a new-born baby

2. Preparation for the Birth

Read the story of the journey to Bethlehem and the birth of Jesus, Luke 2.1-7.

Mary and Joseph had to leave their home and go to Bethlehem at the time of Jesus' birth. Discuss with the children what provision Mary and Joseph had to make in the stable for the birth of Jesus - the manger, the clean straw, the swaddling clothes and warmth.

Encourage the children to consider the needs of the child for shelter, food and clothes. Ask them to make a list of what their mother would need if she were about to give birth. If possible ask a new mother to come to the session with a suitcase full of the things she would need for a new-born baby.

3. Response to the Birth

Read the story of the visit of the shepherds and wise men, Luke 2.8-20, Matthew 2.1-11.

Ask the children what they feel when they see a new-born baby. Like the shepherds at the manger many children have a sense of wonder at a new-born child. There is also the sense of hope and expectancy for a new baby.

When a baby is born people often send cards and presents to greet the new child and congratulate the parents. At Christmas we give gifts as a reminder that God gave the gift of Jesus. Christmas is an appropriate time to explore the theme of gift-giving with children. Ask them what they would bring for a new-born baby. If possible the teacher should bring in some examples of gifts. In the Christmas story the men from the East bring precious gifts for the Christ-child. Gifts need not be expensive or large. They are a token expression of our thanks and love. Discuss with the children what makes a gift valuable. A specially made Christmas card like the one described below can be a precious gift to someone.

CRAFT SUGGESTIONS

A Christ child baby album

Young children might like to make their own Jesus Baby Album. This can either be an album produced by the whole class with drawings done by the children of the Christmas story as seen by Mary and Joseph, or it could be an individual scrapbook which includes newspaper accounts of the census in Bethlehem, the sighting of a bright star etc.

A Christmas card/gift

This paper nativity crib can be a Christmas card or gift for the children to make for someone special. With younger children the teacher might need to fold the card and cut out the stable door before the session.

1. Fold a sheet of A4 card in half.

2. With the fold towards you cut out the stable opening as shown in figure 1 and reserve the cut out.

3. Around the stable opening draw the wise men and shepherds - up to two-thirds of the vertical size. Colour in the rest of the outside of the stable and cut away the top corners of the scene to make a roof line. See figure 1.

4. Unfold the card and on the reverse score a line about 5cm away from the centre fold. Fold up along the scored line to make the stable back.

5. Take the piece of card cut out to make the stable opening and fold back the bottom to make a 1cm flap. Draw a picture of Mary, Joseph and the infant Jesus on this shape and cut around their figures. See figure 2.

6. Colour the stable inside.

7. On the reverse of the card the children can write their greeting. See figure 3.

8. Glue the base flap of the nativity family behind the stable opening. Stick the front and back roof edges together to complete the 3-dimensional crib scene. See figure 4.

fig 1
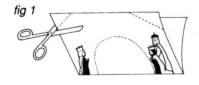

fig 2
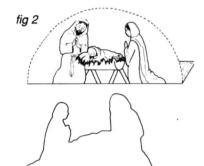

fig 3

fig 4

Epiphany

The Last Act of the Christmas Drama

Andrea Mantegna: The Adoration of the Magi. Bridgeman Art Library, London.

The drama of the Christmas story concludes with the spectacle of the wise men from the East (Matthew 2.1-13). Woven together in this dramatic tapestry are the exotic and mysterious, the evil and the good, suspense and climax. No-one is quite sure who these men were who journeyed from the East following a star. The wise men are not certain whom they seek but they know that he is King of the Jews. The evil King Herod knows nothing of the new king but sets the wise men a trap to ensure that he finds out about any threat to his power. The climax of the story comes when the wise men find the child Jesus with Mary and offer him precious gifts which symbolise his kingship. They fall down and worship him. Herod's evil plans are thwarted as the visitors are warned in a dream not to return to him. The wise men then disappear without trace from the Gospel narrative.

ACTIVITY IDEAS

Themes

Matthew's account of the visit of the wise men is an excellent story to explore in drama. By making their own theatre and playing out the story children can appreciate the drama of the occasion. The finished performance can form part of an Epiphany service or party.

Timing

This activity takes at least two sessions. During the first session the children make the theatre and scenery. In the second session they make the characters and play out the drama. Alternatively the activity could be used as an afternoon workshop. If time is limited the teacher could cut out the cardboard box to make the theatre in advance of the session.

To make the theatre

* Cut the top flaps off the box and keep them to one side.

* Make a stage opening and cut out the sides of the box as shown.

* In order to hang the scenery make three grooves on either side of the top of the box.

* Paint the front of the stage and the floor.

* Attach the stage curtain to a garden cane and slot into the front set of grooves.

The scenery

Before making the scenery read the story of the wise men to the whole group. The story can be divided into three scenes:

Scene 1   The wise men see the star and travel to Jerusalem

Scene 2   The palace of Herod

Scene 3   The house at Bethlehem

Divide the children into three groups of mixed ages to make the three sets for the story. Discuss with them how they can illustrate the stage sets by making a backdrop and a pair of wings to go at the sides.

You will need

cardboard box

scissors

ruler

pencil

trimming knife

paints and paintbrushes

household cloth or material to make a stage curtain

garden cane the same width as the stage opening

sticky tape

Give each group a pair of wings and a backdrop. Two pairs of wings can be cut from the sides of the cardboard box and the third cut from the top flaps of the theatre box. The backdrops are taken from the front, back and bottom of the cardboard box.

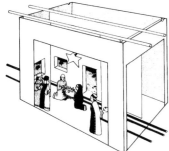

* The children can paint their scenes on the backdrop and wings.

* Attach the backdrop to a cane with sticky tape and the two wings to a separate cane.

* Try the scenery in the grooves.

The characters

Re-tell the Epiphany story to the group. On a large sheet of paper ask the children to write down which characters appear in each scene of the story. Divide the children into the same three groups as before to make the three sets of characters required.

Scene 1	Wise men standing and pointing to a star in the sky
	The star
	Wise men on camels with servants and luggage
Scene 2	Wise men standing
	Herod on his throne with servants around him
	Chief priests and teachers of the law with books
Scene 3	Wise men kneeling down
	Mary
	Joseph
	Jesus

* Draw the characters on thin card in proportion to the stage set.

* Each character should be coloured in and cut out.

* On the reverse of each character place the end of a pea stick in the middle of the card. Attach to the card with sticky tape. The pea sticks can be attached in a vertical or horizontal position so that the children can play out the drama from the sides or from the top of the theatre.

The drama

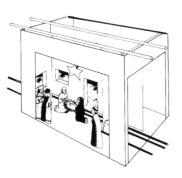

The groups can now narrate a three-scene drama of the Epiphany story using the stage sets and the characters they have made. The characters are worked by moving the pea sticks from the side or the top opening of the theatre. Some groups might want to experiment with lighting by using torches. Others might want to add music or sing Epiphany hymns.

The Conversion of St Paul

JANUARY 25th JANUARY

A fourteenth century picture of St Paul by Ugolino Lorenzetti, now in the Wallraf-Richartz-Museum, Cologne, Germany. St Paul is often illustrated with a thin long face and bearded. He may be depicted with a sword, an attribute referring to his martyrdom, or with a book or scroll of his Epistles.

St Paul may be remembered on two days in the calendar. The Feast of the Conversion of St Paul is on 25 January. The Apostle also shares a day with St Peter on 29 June.

More is known about the life, work and theology of St Paul than any other character in the Bible. He was born in Tarsus in Cilicia, into a Hellenistic Jewish family of the tribe of Benjamin. He enjoyed the status of Roman citizen. We know from Acts that he was brought up a Pharisee (Acts 26.5), was educated in Jerusalem (Acts 22.3), and had a thorough knowledge of Judaism and the Law. Acts also records that Paul persecuted the first Christians and assisted at the martyrdom of St Stephen (Acts 7.58). It was after this, during a mission to Damascus to arrest some Christians that he was converted. No other conversion in the Bible is so dramatic or so well attested (Acts 9.1-19, 22.6-16, 26.12-18).

ACTIVITY IDEAS

Themes

The teacher should first read the story of the conversion of St Paul to the children. The children can mime or act out the story as the teacher reads.

Younger children might find the idea of conversion is very abstract but they can appreciate the drama of the story by understanding what it means to be suddenly made blind. Activity 1 explores the sudden blindness experienced by St Paul and his need to trust in people.

Older children can explore the theme of hearing God. Activity 2 looks at how different people in the Bible have heard God's call and how it is heard today.

Timing

Activity 1 takes one session. Activity 2 may take one or two sessions.

1. Trusting in God
(younger children)

"Saul arose from the ground; and when his eyes were opened he could see nothing. So they led him by the hand and brought him into Damascus." (Acts 9.8 RSV)

Younger children can begin to understand what it means to be suddenly made blind by playing well-known blindfold games such as blind man's buff. After they have done this talk to them about how blind people rely on their other senses because they cannot see. Although St Paul was blinded by his experience on the road to Damascus, he clearly heard the word of God and he had to trust his companions to help him. This idea of listening to God and trusting in his people is central to the conversion story. Children can appreciate something of this trust by playing this game.

An action dice game

You will need

4 roll boxes from aluminium foil etc.

strips of paper

glue

felt pens

blindfold

The teacher might find it easier to make one action dice before the session.

To make an action dice:

1. Write four simple instructions on four strips of paper.

2. Stick these onto four faces of a long cardboard box. See diagram. (The teacher should ensure that two of these instructions are difficult for a blindfolded child to carry out, e.g. - Walk to the door. Go to the toilet. Clap your hands. Touch your toes).

3. Make four action dice.

To play the game the teacher should roll one box and get all the class to do the action which is uppermost on the box. Then blindfold one child and ask the other children to roll each of the four boxes in turn, reading out the instructions so there is a series of four commands. The blindfolded child has to carry out these instructions in order. Each child needs to have a turn at being blindfolded.

When everyone has been blindfolded ask the children how they felt about the actions they had to carry out. Did anyone help them do the actions? If not play the game so someone helps the blindfolded child. Then ask the blindfolded child whether they found it easy to trust their friend.

2. Hearing God's Call
(older children)

The Call of God in the Bible

Children may be puzzled about how God calls people. In the case of St Paul it was dramatic and clear. Get the children to explore other biblical stories where God calls people to his special tasks.

> God calling to Moses out of the burning bush. Exodus 3

> God calling to Samuel. 1 Samuel 3

> Jesus calls to disciples. Matthew 4. 18-22

Children can act out these incidents.

The Call of God today

Once the teacher has explored the biblical understanding of a call from God they need to explore how we hear God's word today. For some people this is a direct call which they hear, for others it is a call from the heart, or from their conscience. If possible the teacher could tell a story of how they have felt

You will need

Bibles

pictures of war and famine, etc.

card

scissors

drawing materials

magazines and newspapers

glue

paper

called to do something because of their belief. Alternatively, the teacher could tell the story of someone else who has felt the call of God - e.g. Cliff Richard, Archbishop Desmond Tutu, Terry Waite, Mother Teresa, etc.

Discussion ideas

The teacher can then show the pictures of war, famine, etc. and discuss them with the children. Some people hear God calling them to do something about the problems which face our planet today. With each picture ask the children what they think God might be saying to them.

Once the children have looked at how God calls us to work in his world ask them to consider more personal experiences. Ask them to think about the last 24 hours. Were there occasions when they could see God at work, or when they felt that they should have done something but didn't?

A card triptych

A practical activity which draws the Old Testament story, the conversion of St Paul and the children's own experience together is a card triptych.

1. Divide a piece of card into three and score down the folds so that it can stand unsupported.

2. Draw a picture of the conversion of St Paul in the centre panel.

3. Draw one of the Old Testament stories they have discussed or acted out in the left hand panel.

4. Draw a picture or make a collage of something they believe God calls them to do today in the right hand panel.

The children might want to add words or a prayer to each of their drawings.

This triptych can then provide a focus for the children's prayers and act as a reminder of the lesson.

Candlemas

A Light to the World

FEBRUARY · 2nd · FEBRUARY

Candlemas is also known by two other names - the Purification of the Blessed Virgin Mary and the Presentation of Christ at the Temple. The three titles give a clue to the three things being remembered on 2 February - the recollection of the prophecy of Simeon in the Temple that the infant Jesus would be "a light for revelation to the Gentiles, and for glory to thy people Israel" (Luke 2. 22-39), the Jewish rites surrounding childbirth for women (Leviticus 12. 6) and the presentation and offering of a first-born Jewish child to God for His service.

The feast was first celebrated in Jerusalem in the fourth century. In 542 the Emperor Justinian ordered its observance at Constantinople as a thanksgiving after a plague and then the custom spread through the East. The introduction of a procession with candles is believed to have originated with Pope Sergius I (687-701). At Candlemas some churches bless all the candles which will be used during the year.

Stained glass window at Hillingdon Hospital Chapel by Jane Gray: the central flame of the seven-branched candlestick from The Revelation of St John the Divine

ACTIVITY IDEAS

Themes

These activities for Candlemas focus on the prophecy of Simeon in the Temple that Jesus would be "a light for revelation to the Gentiles".

Resources

If you plan to organise a Candlemas procession or have a special service on this day you should refer to *The Promise of His Glory: Services and Prayers for the Season from All Saints to Candlemas* (CHP/Mowbray). This gives a full exploration of all the themes of the season and worship suggestions.

Timing

These activities can take one or two sessions.

Exploring the Theme of Light

Read Luke 2. 22-39 from a children's Bible to remind the children what Candlemas celebrates. Darken a room and then light one baptismal candle in the centre of the room.

Remind the children of the point in the baptism service when the priest gives a lighted candle to the person baptised and says, "Receive this light, this is to show that you have passed from darkness to light." Then remind them of the congregation's response, "Shine as a light in the world to the glory of God the Father."

Explore the imagery of light with the children. Ask them what light is for and make a list. Then go through the list and ask them why Christians describe Jesus as a light: e.g. Light helps things to grow; Jesus helps us grow nearer to God; Lights light up a dark path or road; Jesus shows us the way. In the baptism service Christians are exhorted to "shine as a light in the world." How can we shine?

Once you have explored this imagery the group can then choose one of the following activities.

1. A Candle Card

To make the candle holder:

1. Cut out a piece of card 7cm square for the base of the holder.

2. Cut out a piece of card 14cm x 12cm and score in half. Attach this to the base with sticky tape. See diagram.

You will need

night lights

matches

card

sticky tape

glue

drawing materials

paper

Blu-Tack

3. Give each child two sheets of paper 7cm x 12cm. Ask the children to draw a picture of themselves on one sheet and a picture of Jesus on the other.

4. Stick these pictures on the inside of the candle holder.

5. Blu-Tack the night light on the base of the candle holder.

 When lit the candle cards remind the children that they, like Jesus, are to be lights of the world.

2. A Church of Stained Glass Windows

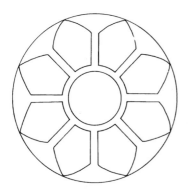

A rose window

You will need

large cardboard boxes

scissors

greaseproof paper

felt pens

sticky tape

torches

paint and drawing materials

Before the session the teacher needs to cut out 'windows' in a large cardboard box. Cut out one window for each child and prepare sheets of greaseproof paper slightly larger than the windows.

To make the church:

1. Give each child a piece of the greaseproof paper to make a stained glass window. They should use black felt pen to create the lead tracing. The stained glass can be created by drawing shapes in brightly coloured felt pens.

2. Once completed these windows can be taped lightly inside the cardboard box holes.

3. Decorate the box as a church.

Remind the children that Christians are to shine as lights in the world just as the church windows shine at night. To illustrate this in a simple way darken the room and put lit torches in the cardboard box so the children can see the church and stained glass windows light up. When the session is nearly over you can dismantle the windows and give each child their own window to take home to display to remind them that they are "lights in the world".

St David

Patron Saint of Wales

Statue of St David at St David's Cathedral, Dyfed

The life of St David is surrounded by rich legend. All we definitely know about him is that he was Welsh, a monk, a bishop and that he lived in the sixth century.

St David or Dewi was a saint of Pembrokeshire (Dyfed) on the south-western tip of Wales. After the Saxon invasion, Christians in the west and north of Britain developed closer links with Christians in Ireland, Gaul and other Celtic communities. From Gaul came the monastic movement which spread and flourished in Wales. There were so many Welsh religious leaders in the fifth and sixth centuries that this period became known as the 'Age of the Saints'.

Although St David is the most popular Welsh saint, the earliest written account of his life that survives dates from long after his death. The first mention of him comes from two Irish lists of martyrs compiled in the ninth and tenth centuries. In about 1090 Rhigyfarch wrote a detailed biography which survives to this day in the British Museum.

According to Rhigyfarch, David was born into a noble family and his mother was Non, later to become a saint herself. David was first educated at Hen Fynyw and then studied for 10 years as a priest under St Paulinus the Welsh scribe. Rhigyfarch says that David founded 12 monasteries including Menevia, today's St David's, and Glastonbury. David settled at Menevia where the monks lived in extreme hardship following the example of those in Egypt. They tilled the land by hand plough, were allowed to speak only when necessary, and ate only bread, vegetables and salt. David's nickname was Aquaticus because he and his monks drank only water.

Rhigyfarch says that David was called to the Synod of Brevi, the modern Llanddewi Brefi. Here he is said to have spoken with such grace that he was unanimously elected primate of the Cambrian church. David died at his monastery at Menevia and his relics are believed to be in St David's Cathedral, Dyfed. There is a very ancient tradition that he died on a Tuesday, 1 March. This date fell on a Tuesday in the year 589. His festival was certainly kept on 1 March from early times.

ACTIVITY IDEAS

Themes

A good starting point for activities on St David is the *Collect* printed here. This draws together the themes of the suggested activities - giving thanks for the life and work of St David, and building on the foundations he made.

"Grant, O Lord, that as we give thanks for the life and work of your servant David, so your Church in Wales may faithfully preach the gospel which he proclaimed, and build on the foundation which he laid; through Jesus Christ our Lord."

(The Cloud of Witnesses)

Resources

Teachers may find the following books useful:

The Opened Door - A Celtic Spirituality by Patrick Thomas (Silyn Publications, Brechfa 1990)

Celtic Crosses of Britain and Ireland by Malcolm Seaborne (Shire Archaeology series)

Leaflets and brochures are available from St David's Cathedral

Timing

Activity 1 provides worship suggestions: one session is needed for preparation and one for the service. Activity 2a can be done in one session and activities 2b and 2c are suggested as simple alternatives to 2a.

1. Giving Thanks for the Life and Work of St David

(all-age activity)

St David is remembered for his preaching and teaching. He is the patron saint of a country renowned for its choirs, singers, musicians and poets. After hearing the story of St David children can be encouraged to prepare a special celebration service with a Welsh theme to give thanks for the life of St David.

The week before the celebration bring a selection of hymn books, song books, musical instruments and poetry books to the session and ask the children to find material which has a Welsh character. Discuss with them what could be included in a service.

You will need

hymn books and song books

poetry books

musical instruments

dressing up clothes

Get the children to consider how St David preached the gospel. Discuss the type of austere life that St David lived. The children could then create a drama around St David preaching the gospel to pagans. This could form part of the service.

The service could also include or focus on the Celtic cross made in the following activity.

2. Building on the Foundation - the Celtic Cross

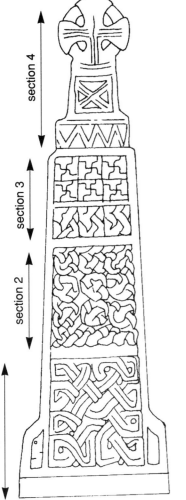

The Carew Cross

The cross is now the universal symbol of Christianity but it was some centuries before it became a popular symbol. Simple crosses carved on stones in Wales date back to the time of St David. These crosses showed that Christianity was established in an area. They might also have marked graves, a precinct of a monastery or a place associated with the founder of a particular monastery. Later crosses became more elaborate, free standing with carved intricate detail on the cross shape. Celtic sculptors were influenced by Irish, English and later Viking art forms. The Carew Cross, standing near the entrance of Carew Castle in Dyfed, illustrated here, is an excellent example of an eleventh-century cross. These activities can help remind children that the crosses they see around the British countryside are linked to the foundation of the Christian faith on these islands.

You will need

two large sheets of cardboard

photocopies of the cross illustrated

felt pens

wools

scissors

stones

glue

a) In advance of the session take the two sheets of cardboard to draw a copy of the cross illustrated. Draw the design in felt pen. Aim to have the cross as near to life size as possible (14ft). Cut out the different sections of pattern.

The older children can take sections one and two of the cross and stick coloured string or wool onto the design following the continuous lines.

Remind the group that the unbroken lines on Celtic crosses are said to symbolise eternity and the continuity of God's love.

Section three can be divided into smaller squares and each square be given to a younger child to stick pre-cut wools onto the pattern areas. When the sections are completed they can be stuck onto a complete card cross and used as a focus for worship.

b) Photocopy enough copies of the crosses for children to colour in individually. Cut them out and stick them onto card for the children to use as bookmarks for their Bibles.

c) The children can copy some of the shapes on the Carew Cross, or other cross shapes, onto small stones.

St Patrick

Patron Saint of Ireland

St Patrick's window in Magheralin Parish Church.
Northern Ireland Tourist Board

There are many stories about the patron saint of Ireland. Some are true, some are legend and some have a touch of the blarney about them. We can be sure however that we are hearing the real St Patrick when we read his *Confession* and *Letter to Coroticus*, which are believed by scholars to originate from the saint himself.

Patrick was born between AD 390 and AD 414, possibly in modern Cumbria. He was the son of a local town councillor called Calpurnius who was a churchman and deacon. When Patrick was sixteen he was captured by Irish pirates who took him to work on a farm near "the woods of Foclut by the western seas" probably in County Mayo. After the relative comfort of his home the shock of working as a shepherd in a remote country had a profound effect on Patrick. He believed that he deserved his banishment because "we turned away from God, and did not keep his commandments". In his loneliness Patrick came to know God as a friend and companion and later recalled that he said as many as a hundred prayers every day.

During this time Patrick received a message from God that was to change his life. He heard a voice say "Your ship is ready". Patrick was puzzled since being in Western Ireland he was then at the furthest point of Europe. He travelled 200 miles East and then set sail for England where after various adventures he became ordained. His *Confession* recounts a series of dreams and visions, the most significant being a call to return to Ireland to serve its people.

In about 435 he returned there as Bishop and gradually he gained the trust of kings and ordinary people. Local chieftains entrusted their children to him so that he could educate them and these pupils travelled with Patrick as he went around Ireland evangelising, ordaining clergy and setting up religious houses for monks and nuns.

Although Patrick was not a scholar himself, he had a sincere simplicity of life and a deep pastoral care for all he met. Legends about him are plentiful and there are memoirs, biographies, hymns and unwritten traditions which link Patrick with people and places all over Ireland.

ACTIVITY IDEAS

Themes

Throughout his life Patrick relied on his prayer life to sustain him in his difficulties and adventures. These activities are designed so that children can understand more about the way St Patrick depended on prayer. They utilise two things traditionally associated with him, the prayer *St Patrick's Breastplate* and the shamrock.

Resources

If possible get a copy of the *Confession* so that older children can read part of it for themselves. The text reveals a great deal about Patrick's character. There are also many books about him. Try to find one that is based on the *Confession* rather than later lives about him; particularly useful are *The Real Story of Patrick* by George Otto Simms, published by The O'Brien Press 1991, and *The Cry of the Deer: Meditations on the Hymn of St Patrick* by David Adam, Triangle 1987.

Timing

Each activity takes one session.

PRAYER

Christ be with me, Christ within me,

Christ behind me, Christ before me,

Christ beside me, Christ to win me,

Christ to comfort and restore me,

Christ beneath me, Christ above me,

Christ in quiet, Christ in danger,

Christ in hearts of all that love me,

Christ in mouth of friend and stranger.

(C.F. Alexander's translation)

---

1. St Patrick's Breastplate

Nearly 500 years after his death a life of Patrick was written in Irish called *The Tripartite Life*. It contains the text of a prayer which has been associated ever since with St Patrick. It is known as *St Patrick's Breastplate*, the *Lorica of St Patrick* or *The Deer's Cry* and is found in many hymnbooks. Although most scholars agree that it was not written by the saint himself the words in it echo what Patrick writes about in his *Confessions* concerning the immediacy of God .

Before the session make a paper or card breastplate for each child as shown in the illustration. You will find that paper breastplates need the corner holes reinforcing with sticky tape. Thread string through the breastplates as shown. If there is time the children can make their own breastplates.

You will need

copies of the prayer

paper or card breastplates for each child

string

sticky tape

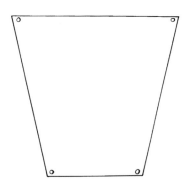

DISCUSSION QUESTIONS

* How is Jesus in them and around them all the time?

* How do they turn to Jesus in danger?

* Do they think that Jesus is in someone they know?

* Can they think of times when people speak out in the name of Jesus?

* Why do they think the prayer is called St Patrick's Breastplate?

At the beginning of the session sing or read together the prayer with the children. Then ask them the questions.

After the discussion give each child a paper breastplate. Ask them to write out each phrase of the prayer given here on one side of the breastplate. Then ask them to think about each phrase in turn. On the second half of the paper breastplate they can continue each phrase to make St Patrick's prayer their own.

eg   Christ be with me ... *when I get up in the morning.*

        Christ within me ... *when I am frightened.*

These breastplates can serve as a reminder to the children that God is their protector just as he looked after St Patrick.

2. A Shamrock Badge

The linking of St Patrick with the three-leaved shamrock first appears in written form in the eighteenth century. The shamrock has since then become the unofficial emblem of Ireland.

Read the baptismal creed on page 247 of the ASB. Explain to the children that this creed is said by godparents and parents for children at their baptism. Remind them that a creed is a statement of what someone believes.

Throughout Christian history people have used pictures or symbols to describe God. The shamrock with its three leaves springing from one stem provides a visual reminder of St Patrick's teaching on the Trinity. "This word picture of God as three persons in one was used by him to explain to his followers that God's love was shown first when he created the world, second, when Jesus Christ came into the world, and third, through the Holy Spirit whose love and power works among all people's of the world." (George Otto Simms, *The Real Story of Patrick*, p.48)

You will need

copies of the *Alternative Service Book*

card

sticky tape

safety pins

colouring materials

Children can make their own shamrock badge for St Patrick's Day on 17 March. Using the template cut out a shamrock shape on card. The children can then write the words Father, Son, Holy Spirit in the three parts of the leaf to remind them of Patrick's teaching on the Trinity. Secure a safety pin at the back of the card with sticky tape to make a badge.

At the end of the session recite the baptismal creed and ask the group to give the responses.

Mothering Sunday

*La mère et l'enfant by David
Silverberg*

Mothering Sunday, which provides a welcome 'time off' from Lent, brings together a glorious array of traditions. Its roots lie in ancient Rome, its customs belong to 18th century Britain and its commercial success is due largely to the American armed forces.

The Romans honoured their goddess of motherhood in Spring with the feast of Matronalia. Cakes made of special extra-fine flour known as simila were baked and offered to her. When the Church became established in Britain Christians incorporated these customs, but instead of celebrating Matronalia they honoured Mother Church.

It is unclear when the honouring of Mother Church was extended to include thanksgiving for our own mothers. During the 18th and 19th centuries Mothering Sunday was a day when domestic servants were given time off to visit their own homes and mothers. They would often take special presents including a Simnel cake. The Simnel cake may owe its name to the white floured cakes offered at Matronalia. Others claim a Shropshire origin for it.

Mother's Day arrived in England when American armed forces were based here during World War II. They brought with them their May customs of honouring their mothers with gifts of cards, flowers and sweets. Today Mothering Sunday and Mother's Day are celebrated on the fourth Sunday of Lent. Mothering Sunday is also sometimes called Refreshment Sunday, or Laetare Sunday, traditionally a day when the fasting rules of Lent are relaxed.

Throughout history Mothering Sunday has been a remarkably adaptable festival. Its themes of mothering, caring, and giving thanks are universal. Today some churches concentrate on the concept of 'mothering' and instead of focusing only on Mother Church and our own mothers, emphasise the 'mothering' everyone does at home or in the community.

ACTIVITY IDEAS

Themes

The central theme of Mothering Sunday is thanksgiving for Mother Church and our own mothers. These activities concentrate on the latter. The modern teacher obviously has to be sensitive to the family circumstances of their group. In some groups it might be more appropriate to talk about carers.

Food and flowers are the traditional Mothering Sunday gifts. These activities are designed to adapt the traditional customs.

First ask the children to consider what their mothers or carers do for them. Ask the questions, "Why do we give thanks to God for our mother? What does she do for us?" Each child can be encouraged to compose a simple prayer thanking God for their mother.

Once the theme of thanksgiving has been explored the teacher can then consider the symbolism of giving gifts. Explain to the children that gifts are a symbol of love, thanksgiving and celebration. Just as their own mother loves them and takes time and care over them, they can now take time and care to produce a gift which represents their love for their mother.

Timing

These activities are designed for a single session.

1. Foil Basket (younger children)

You will need

small foil pie dishes

card

scissors

colouring and sticking materials

staples

small sweets or biscuits

A simple small basket can be quickly made by stapling a card handle to a small foil pie dish. The handle can be decorated by the children before it is stapled on. The basket can then be filled with sweets or biscuits.

2. Flower Arrangement
(older children)

Before the session the teacher needs to cut enough oases to fit the insides of the plastic lids. Each piece of oasis should be twice the height of the rim of a lid. To make the arrangement:

* Secure the dry oasis to the bottom of the lid with Blu-Tack.

* Wet the oasis.

* Cut out two heart shapes from decorative paper.

* Take the florist's wire and sandwich the heart shapes at the top of the wire as shown in the illustration.

* Draw a smaller heart on white paper and ask the children to write a message or poem to their mothers.

* Stick this on the paper heart on the florist's wire.

* Put the wire through the oasis into the Blu-Tack.

* Around this base the children can arrange flowers, evergreens, or paper flowers.

You will need

plastic lids

flower oasis

Blu-Tack

flowers

decorative paper

florist's wire

white paper

drawing materials

scissors

3. Pop-up Mothering Sunday Card

To make the peacock card the children need to:

* Fold a rectangle of card measuring approximately 15cm x 20cm.

* Decorate the front of the card for a Mothering Sunday card.

* Inside the card draw the back of a peacock in the centre.

* Cut out a strip of paper measuring 5cm by 30cm and draw the outline of a peacock pattern.

* Pleat this strip. Then glue the strip at each end and place in the centre of the card to form a peacock tail.

* The wording inside the card can include something like, "I'm proud that you are my Mum" or "I'm proud to be your son".

You will need

card

scissors

paper

colouring materials

glue

Easter

Celebrating the Drama of the Resurrection

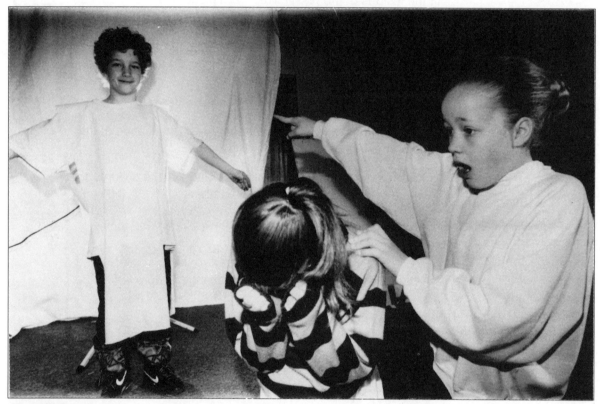

The Nazareth Youth Theatre, Lancaster, in a performance of an Easter drama, The Man from Luke. Photograph: Dave Clark

The celebration of the resurrection of Christ is the greatest and the oldest festival in the Church. It is the commemoration of Christ's victory of life over death. In the Western Church Easter Day falls on the Sunday following the first full moon after the spring equinox.

The name Easter probably owes its origins to the ancient spring goddess "Eostre". The church historian Bede thought that this was so, and it is clear that in Britain the Christian festival superseded an old pagan festival.

Many Easter customs pre-date Christianity. The giving of eggs originates from ancient China where eggs symbolised the return of spring and the continuance of life. For Christians they became a symbol of the resurrection of Christ and a new life in him.

ACTIVITY IDEAS

Themes, Resources and Timing

There are plenty of books full of activity ideas on eggs, bunnies and hats. Particularly useful is *Bright Ideas - Easter* by Jim Fitzsimmons (Scholastic Publications). The activities suggested here concentrate on the Easter story itself.

The first activity is a Bible study/drama and could be incorporated into a family service or two sessions. This activity needs to be adapted to suit the local conditions. Scenery and costumes are optional. What is important is that the children experience something of what it was like to be there on the first Easter morning.

The second activity for younger children uses the idea of a flowering Easter branch. This flowering branch can also form part of a service or be planted in an Easter garden in the drama. This activity takes one session.

1. An Easter Drama

Bible study

Each of the four evangelists gives an account of the Easter story: Matthew 28.1-10, Mark 16.1-11, Luke 24.1-12, John 20.1-24. If possible divide the children into four groups. Give each group a large sheet of paper and ask them to look at one of the passages and to read it out.

On the paper the children should write down the names of the people who appear in the account they have been given. They should record the experiences, feelings and speech of each person in their text.

Retelling the story

The groups should then come together and discuss the characters involved in their account. Do not worry about the obvious differences in the accounts. Eyewitnesses of any incident will tell of their experience in a different way. Concentrate on feelings which the characters might have experienced - surprise, fear, joy, and trepidation.

To help the children to appreciate the characters and the sequence of events on the first Easter morning ask them the questions.

DISCUSSION QUESTIONS

* What other stories in the Bible do they know about the characters they have chosen?

* Why had the body been put hurriedly into the tomb?

* Why do they think the women met early in the morning?

Once the children have had a full discussion about the people involved in the Easter story and the sequence of events they can go back into their smaller groups to rehearse a role play.

Alternatively if the group wants to perform a single drama then they can come together again as a larger group and decide for themselves which version to perform.

2. A Flowering Easter Branch
(younger children)

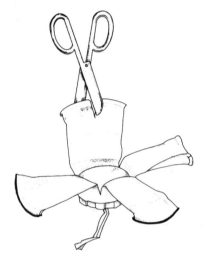

It is a common custom at Easter time to take a few branches of a budding tree into the home and decorate it with coloured eggs for Easter. In some places the twigs are put into a cross shape. The flowering branch then serves as a reminder that the cross led to new life in Jesus. This tradition can be adapted for young children. They can each make their own Easter flower to attach to a branch and remind them that Jesus was raised from death at Easter for everyone.

To make the flowering branch:

* Draw around the base of the cup on coloured paper and cut out a circle shape.

* The petals are made by cutting five slits down from the rim to the base of the cup as shown in the illustration.

* Gently bend back the petals.

* Write on the petals with a soft pencil or permanent felt pen: Jesus was raised for me.

* Ask each child to write their name on the coloured circle and stick this onto the base of the cup to form the flower's centre.

* Using sticky tape attach the end of the wire bag tie to the back of the flower.

* The flowers can then be hooked to the branches.

Remind the children that through the death of Jesus on Good Friday we have forgiveness of sins. He was raised to life on Easter day so that everyone can have new life in him. The flowers on the tree serve as a reminder of this new life.

You will need

white plastic cups

yellow coloured paper

sticky tape

wire bag ties

glue

scissors

branch in pot

soft pencil

permanent felt pen

St George

Patron Saint of England

APRIL · **23**rd · APRIL

*Paulo Uccello: Saint George
and the Dragon.
Reproduced by courtesy
of the Trustees,
The National Gallery, London*

St George has captured the imagination and hearts of Christians in both the Eastern and Western Churches although little is actually known about him.

It is likely that he lived in the fourth century and suffered martyrdom near Lydda (Diospolis in Palestine) before the time of the Emperor Constantine. It is possible that he was a soldier. By the sixth century St George had become a popular saint. Plentiful legends about him survive in Greek, Latin, Armenian, Coptic, Syriac, Ethiopian and Turkish.

The dragon story first appears in the twelfth century and is recounted in the thirteenth-century *Golden Legend*, a manual of the lives of the saints which was translated and printed by Caxton. The dragon was a local pest that terrorized the whole country. Its breath was said to poison all who approached it. Its daily diet was two sheep but when the country ran out of sheep, human victims were offered instead. One day the lot fell on the king's daughter. She went to the dragon to meet her fate dressed as a bride. At this point St George appeared. Single-handedly he attacked the dragon and pierced it with his sword. St George then made a lead from the princess's girdle and led the dragon through the town for all to see. The people were terrified but St George reassured them by saying that he would kill the dragon if all the town were baptised. The king and all his subjects agreed. Fifteen thousand people were baptised and the dragon was slain.

No one is quite certain how St George came to be the patron saint of England. He became particularly popular in England during the Crusades since he personified the ideal of Christian chivalry and was adopted as the patron saint of soldiers. Richard 1 placed himself and his army under the saint's protection. Edward III made George patron of the Order of the Garter. At the battle of Agincourt Henry V invoked St George as England's patron. Although St George has often become the symbol of English nationalism he is also patron of Venice, Genoa, Portugal, Istanbul, and Catalonia.

ACTIVITY IDEAS

Themes

Never miss a good story. The tale of St George and the dragon is part of our heritage and still has relevance today. This classic adventure story shows how good triumphs over evil. The aim of the following activities is to help children take part in the story of St George through drama and then to consider the modern 'dragons' or wrongs we have to fight against today.

Timing

Activity 1, the drama, needs at least one session, preferably two. Activity 2 takes one session and can follow on from activity 1.

1. The Drama

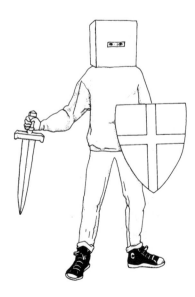

Divide the children into two groups, the St George group and the dragon group.

The *St George* group needs to make a shield, a sword and a helmet. They can make a shield from part of a cardboard box painted with the red St George cross on a white background. The sword can also be made from card and decorated. Make the helmet from a cardboard box or a brown paper shopping bag with handles.

The *dragon* group can make the head of the dragon from a decorated cardboard box. Cut off the bottom flaps from the box. Cut two sides of the box so that it can fit over the shoulders of a child as shown. Cut holes for the eyes and decorate as a dragon with scrap materials. The body is made

You will need

a belt with which to lead the dragon

2 cardboard boxes

paint

scissors

brown paper carrier bag

plastic carrier bags

card

masking tape

materials for the dragon's head

double sheet

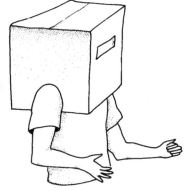

from a double sheet covered with scales cut from plastic carrier bags and stuck on with masking tape. One child is needed for the dragon head and one or two can go under the sheet to make up the body.

The group then needs to choose a princess, a St George and people to dress up as the dragon. They can then act out the story of how St George saves the princess. Any remaining children can act as the townspeople.

2. The Relevance of the Story Today

"Fight valiantly under the banner of Christ against sin, the world, and the devil, and continue his faithful soldier and servant to the end of your life."

(ASB Baptism service)

Today we no longer believe in dragons. It is therefore tempting to discount the story of St George. But the message behind the story of a Christian fighting against evil is relevant today. Remind the children of the exhortation of the congregation at a baptism service to "fight valiantly for Christ". Discuss with the children what "sin, the world and the devil" mean today. What are our modern 'dragons' and what must Christians do to fight them. The children might list bullying, stealing, the nuclear threat, pollution, war, hijacks etc. After the discussion the older children can make up their own drama of their modern St George story.

This idea of modern evils needs to be made appropriate for the younger children. Perhaps you can explore the idea of healthy fear with them. Younger children are told to have a fear of strangers approaching them with offers of sweets and car rides, the dangers of cars and lorries, fireworks, etc. Instead of fighting the dragon as St George did they need to learn how to say "no" clearly. The teacher can then tell short stories which include the dangers listed above. Each short story could end with the question: "And what do you say to that?" The children can shout out: "No we don't want to - it's dangerous."

Pentecost

A Mighty Wind and Tongues of Fire

One of the 'Elements in Salvation' tapestries at St Alban's Cathedral. Fire: God appears in the Burning Bush; Column of cloud and fire leading God's people; God hidden in the fire and smoke on Sinai; Three young men in the burning fiery furnace; The new fire at Easter; The fire of the Holy Spirit at Pentecost.
Photo: Woodmansterne (Jeremy Marks) © St Alban's Cathedral

Almighty God,
who on the day of Pentecost
sent your Holy Spirit to the disciples
with the wind from heaven and in tongues of flame,
filling them with joy and boldness to preach the Gospel:
send us out in the power of the same Spirit
to witness to your truth
and to draw all men to the fire of your love;
through Jesus Christ our Lord.

Collect for Pentecost Sunday (ASB)

The day of Pentecost is recounted in Acts 1.1-4. The writer uses powerful, dynamic language - noise, wind, fire - to describe the coming of the Holy Spirit. The images of wind and fire provide an excellent starting point for an exploration of the meaning of the Holy Spirit with children.

ACTIVITY IDEAS

Themes

These activities explore the imagery of fire and wind. They aim to help children appreciate something of the dramatic power of the Holy Spirit. Pentecost is the birthday of the Church and a time for celebration. Following the experience of the Holy Spirit the disciples went out to preach the good news. These activities are designed to help children catch something of the joy and excitement of the first Pentecost. They can be incorporated into a special church celebration or family service.

Timing

The first activity takes one session. The others might take a little longer. If the group begins with the Bible study allow two sessions.

Bible Study and Discussion

First explore the images of fire and wind with the children.

Fire

Fire is used in other parts of the Bible to illustrate God's presence. Read the story of Moses and the burning bush to the children from Exodus 3. Then read Exodus 13. 21-22 which tells how God led the Israelites from Egypt. Discuss with the children the uses of fire - to heat, to cook, to burn. Also consider the different sorts of fire - a candle, a camp fire, a bonfire, a burning house, a volcano. etc. Get the children to consider where fire may be used in church - the Paschal candle, altar candles, baptism candles and sanctuary lamps.

Wind

Using wind as an image of the power of God is not confined to the New Testament. The common Hebrew word for wind is *rûah*, which can be translated 'spirit' or 'breath' depending on its context. In the Exodus story God is shown to have power over wind, Exodus 10.13, 19. He is also in the breath of life, Psalm 104. 29-30. Early Christian writers referred to the Holy Spirit as the energy of God. Read John 3.8 to the children from a Children's Bible and ask them what the writer means.

In a group ask the children to describe what wind is. Practise making the different sounds wind makes - a gentle wind, a hurricane and a storm. Get the group to consider the many uses of wind as a source of power. Discuss with them when wind can be exciting and when frightening, exhilarating or exhausting. Explain to the children that we cannot see wind but we can see its powerful effects. The Holy Spirit is invisible but its work and power are visible in people's lives.

Before you start the activities with children read them the account of the first Pentecost.

"When the day of Pentecost had come, they were all together in one place. And suddenly a sound came from heaven like the rush of a mighty wind, and it filled all the house where they were sitting. And there appeared to them tongues as of fire, distributed and resting on each one of them. And they were all filled with the Holy Spirit and began to speak in other tongues, as the Spirit gave them utterance." (Acts 2.1-4 RSV)

1. Spinning Flame Top

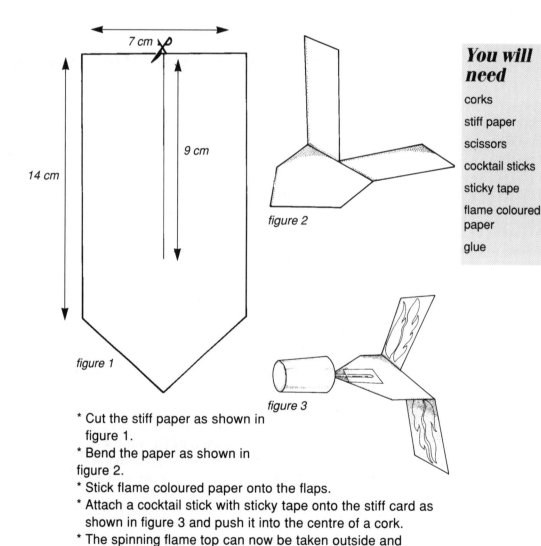

7 cm

9 cm

14 cm

figure 1

figure 2

figure 3

You will need

corks

stiff paper

scissors

cocktail sticks

sticky tape

flame coloured paper

glue

* Cut the stiff paper as shown in figure 1.
* Bend the paper as shown in figure 2.
* Stick flame coloured paper onto the flaps.
* Attach a cocktail stick with sticky tape onto the stiff card as shown in figure 3 and push it into the centre of a cork.
* The spinning flame top can now be taken outside and thrown into the air. The top is spun by the wind to produce a descending fiery flame, a reminder of the first Pentecost.

2. A Wind Sock (older children)

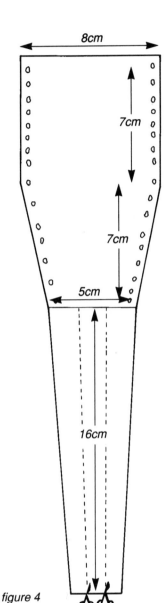

8cm

7cm

7cm

5cm

16cm

figure 4

3cm

* Make a template as shown in figure 4.

* Draw around the template onto three different colours of tissue paper and cut out.

* Cut along the dotted lines to make the fringe.

* To make the sock, overlap the tissue paper along the lines of dots and glue two seams together.

* At the top of the sock glue a strip of card 1cm by 21cm. Form a hoop with the card. Then glue the remaining seam together to complete the sock. Secure the card hoop with a staple. See figure 5.

* Take two lengths of string 18cm long. Make four equidistantly spaced pencil marks in the card hoop. Attach a string end at each pencil mark with sticky tape. You now have two loops of string.

* Gather the two loops together with a long thread of string and attach this string to the pea stick to form the completed wind sock. See figure 5.

The children can now take their wind socks outside and see how powerful the wind is.

You will need

flame coloured tissue paper

strips of card

card template drawn from figure 4

pea sticks

wool or thin string

glue

stapler

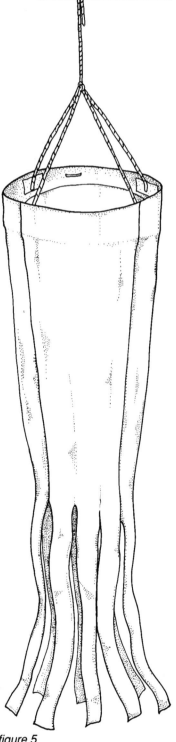

figure 5

Julian of Norwich

The Window in Julian's Cell, St. Julian's Church, Norwich.

The rediscovery of Julian in recent years has produced an enormous interest among devotional readers and scholars alike. The current 'growth industry' stands in stark contrast to the previous 500 years of virtual neglect and to the solitary life she lived as an anchoress.

Little is known about the author of *Revelations of Divine Love*. Julian herself tells us that she received her revelations from God on 8 May 1373 when she was 30 and at the point of death.

Throughout Christian history there have been people who have wanted to withdraw from the world to live a life of prayer. Julian, like many anchorites and anchoresses in the Middle Ages, lived in a cell by a church and it is likely that she took her name from the church. It is unclear whether Julian became an anchoress before or after her religious experience. Her knowledge and sympathy for the care a mother gives a child has led many to suppose that she was a widow. Others presume she was a Benedictine nun.

Julian says that she is 'unlettered' and this has given rise to much debate by modern scholars. Her writings are not only a unique spiritual work but the earliest known writings in English by a woman. She might not have been lettered in Latin, the language of the Church, but it is clear she had received some education and was well versed in scripture.

Julian's influence has been widespread in the 20th century from the small Julian prayer cells to those who champion her as the first feminist theologian. Her writings contain many images which speak clearly to modern Christians. Throughout the Revelations the cross is the central image she uses to show God's love for humankind. Julian was certain, despite the terrible times she lived in, that God is in control: "all shall be well, and all manner of thing shall be well." Julian uses many images to underline the wonder of this love, the most notable of which is her image of God as Mother.

ACTIVITY IDEAS

Themes

These activities aim to help children understand something of Julian's way of life and explore one of the images of God's love that she uses.

Resources

There is a wealth of published material and resources on Julian. Teachers will find the following particularly useful:

Julian of Norwich: Revelations of Divine Love, translated by Clifton Wolters (Penguin Classics)

In Search of Julian of Norwich by Sheila Upjohn (DLT)

Enfolded in Love edited by Robert Llewelyn (DLT)

For children The Julian Shrine Publications produce:

Who was Julian? A beginner's guide by Michael McLean

Julian of Norwich - a Workbook for Schools by N. Groves

These are available from the Julian Centre, St Julian's Alley, Rouen Road, Norwich NR1 1QT.

The Julian Centre and the church are open every day. Talks for groups visiting the Shrine can be arranged by contacting The Warden of the Shrine at the above address.

Timing

Each activity takes two or three sessions. The second activity will need advance planning.

1. A Julian Cell Book

Children may be familiar with monks and nuns but the life of a solitary is more unusual. Remind them that Julian was an anchoress. She stayed in one place like an anchor and lived a life of prayer. Explore the following questions with them:

* How would they feel staying in one room for many years?

* Do they have a special quiet place to say their prayers?

* Do they pray for other people and ask God for things?

"If Julian lived according to the Anchorite Rule, her cell would have had three windows. One would open into the church so she could hear the Mass and receive the sacrament. A second window opened onto an inner room, so that a servant could bring food and clean clothes, and take out the slops. The third window, which was curtained by a black cloth with a white cross at the centre, opened onto the roadway, so the anchoress could look out into the world and speak with people who came in need of her counsel and help."

(Sheila Upjohn: *In Search of Julian of Norwich*)

To help children appreciate how Julian lived they can make their own Julian cell and prayer book.

This model can either be free-standing or be folded into a book. Children can decorate the cell as they wish.

To make the cell:

* Take an A3 sheet of paper and mark up as shown in figure 1.

* Cut out the shaded area to form the roof outline.

* Fold section A and B as shown.

* Reinforce section C with cardboard.

* Turn paper over. Draw two windows (one into the church and one into the street) and a door. Cut these out as shown in figure 2.

* Colour a black curtain with a white cross behind the street window. Draw a figure of Julian behind the door.

* Draw and colour in the outside of the cell.

* Turn over to the inside of the cell. The servant's window can be drawn on the inside of the roof as shown in figure 3. Cut out the window. Underneath draw a picture of the servant.

* The children can then write three sets of prayers:

  1 Along W where the window looks out onto the street the children can write prayers for the world.

  2 Along S which corresponds to the servant's window they can write prayers for those who care for them.

  3 Along P which looks into the church they should write prayers for the church and people. Julian's cell thus becomes full of prayer.

* Assemble cell as shown in figure 4.

* To make the model into a book, concertina the roof and fold away as shown in figure 5. The book will now open out in three different ways to reveal the three sets of prayers.

You will need

cardboard

paper

scissors

colouring materials

pencils and pens

glue

ruler

DISCUSSION QUESTIONS

* What is it that God has made?

* What colour, shape and size is it?

* How does it smell?

* What is its texture?

Help them appreciate the beauty and variety of what God has made.

* Ask them how they think God loves what they have brought?

* How does God look after it?

2. Images of the Love of God: A Nature Display

In her Revelations Julian is shown a little thing by the Lord, the size of a hazelnut in the palm of her hand. In this she saw three truths about the world:

"In this little thing I saw three truths. The first is that God made it; the second is that God loves it; and the third is that God looks after it."

Take the children to a church garden or ask them to bring in from their own garden or the park something from nature which is very small.

The following week discuss with the children what they have found using the questions given.

The children can put their objects on a special table and create a banner saying: God made it. God loves it. God looks after it.

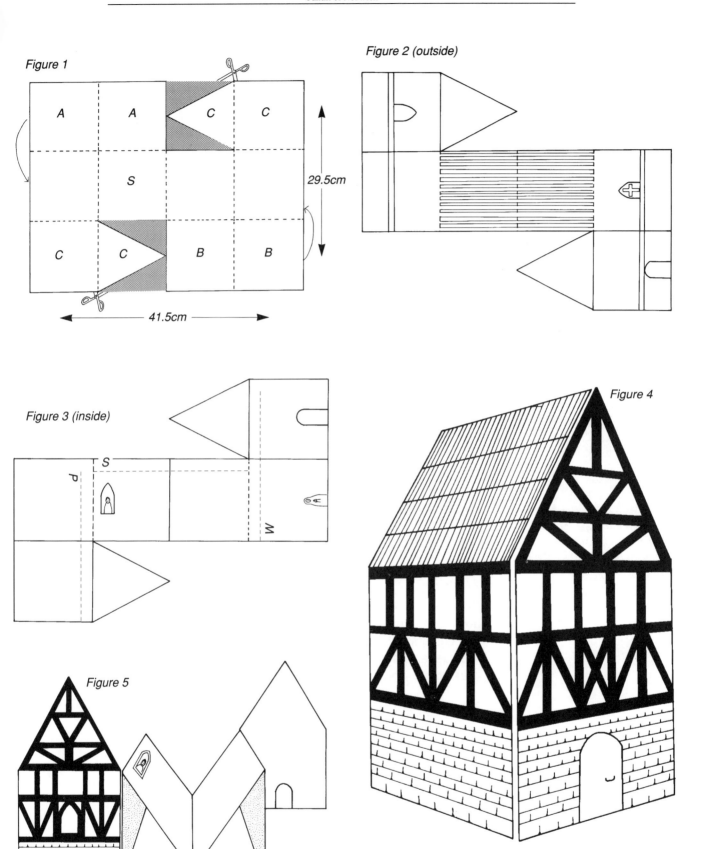

Figure 1

A   A   C   C

S

C   C   B   B

29.5cm

41.5cm

Figure 2 (outside)

Figure 3 (inside)

S

P

W

Figure 4

Figure 5

Christian Aid
Week

Children around the World

*Christian Aid Week 90
Sponsored Canal Walk
Christian Aid/Elaine Dingenan*

C hristian Aid works to combat the poverty and injustice suffered by millions of people around the world. It is an official aid agency of the British and Irish churches and was the first charity to have a special education and fundraising week set aside to focus the public's attention on its work. Each year the theme of the week is different but the aim of the organisation stays the same - to help alleviate poverty without dependency and to strengthen the poor.

ACTIVITY IDEAS

Themes

Christian Aid Week provides an opportunity for children to develop an understanding of why people are poor and to hear and celebrate the stories of people working to improve their lives. It can also be a time for children to reflect on their own lives and to work and pray for a better world.

Resources

These activities can be used in any Christian Aid Week and should be adapted to suit your local situation. Christian Aid also produces special children's material for each year's Christian Aid Week. Contact Christian Aid, P.O. Box 100, London SE1 7RT.

Timing

These activities could be done over one or two sessions in preparation for a Christian Aid Week service.

1. Helping your Neighbour
Bible study

The aim of this exercise is to help children appreciate what it means to be 'in someone else's shoes'. It also helps them understand that helping others or finding the right way of helping others can sometimes be difficult.

Read the story of the Good Samaritan (Luke 10. 29-37). Ask the children to imagine that they are one of the characters in the story and to say how they feel about the situation they are in. Ask the children to act out the story thinking carefully about the role they are given. Act it out a few times so that the children have the chance to play different parts.

After performing the dramas discuss the story with the children:

2. Children Around the World

Stories about children from Brazil, India and Ethiopia have been chosen since these are countries where Christian Aid is involved. Only the bare essentials are given in each case and it is recommended that teachers obtain supplementary material from Christian Aid.

Divide the children into three groups and give them one country each to study. Ask the groups to discuss the questions.

After the discussion each group can do the activity relevant to the children in the country they have learned about. Very young children will enjoy dressing up as children from other countries. Finally the groups can come together to make banners about the countries.

Savithri from India

(a video with notes is available from Christian Aid)

Savithri lives in Pillayanathan in South India. She lives with her mother, grandmother and older sister. Her father left the family because of a dowry dispute. Her family are low status Harijans and are treated with little respect by the higher caste people in the village. Savithri's family are landless so they earn their living as agricultural labourers. Savithri supplements the family income by picking flowers for sale. She attends a state school three miles away. She is also an enthusiastic member of a night school and children's committee. These night schools provide education on health care, the environment, finances, local culture and issues of local concern. The children's committee brings together children from different castes and together they work out how to improve the local community by co-operative effort.

Activity Idea

Encourage the children to make tissue paper flowers. Older children might want to make Indian-type garlands. Remind them that Savithri does this work every day in addition to all her other activities. The completed flowers can be used with the banners in an offertory procession or sold to raise funds for Christian Aid.

Paulo from Brazil

(Further material on Brazil is available from Christian Aid)

Street children in Brazil
Photo: Christian Aid

Paulo lives in Recife in north-east Brazil. Paulo comes from the country but his family had to move to the city when a landowner sold the land where they lived. Paulo lives with his mother and sisters in a small house they built themselves - his mother works in a shop. Paulo and his friends go to a community school which meets in a church hall in the mornings. After school he used to play in the streets but the police would often break up their games saying that they caused trouble. Some of the street children steal or sell drugs to earn money for food. There are between seven and eight million street children in Brazil, many of whom have no family contact. The church gave Paulo and his friends a loan to set up an ice-lolly making shop and let them use the church freezer. After school they go out selling ice-lollies. They have now paid back their loan and with the profit they are making they can buy food for their families.

flowers

Activity Idea

The children can make their own lollies for sale after the Christian Aid Week service. Ask them what they will need to do this and how they could keep the lollies frozen?

Alemitu from Ethiopia

(Christian Aid has an Ethiopia and Eritrea Pack for children)

Alemitu lives in a village in southern Ethiopia. She is nine but until recently could not go to school because she had to collect water with her mother. Twice a day Alemitu used to walk for one-and-a-half hours to get to the river to collect water. People in the village were often sick. One day men came to the village and began digging. A new well was made so Alemitu no longer had to spend 6 hours a day fetching water. The water from the village well is filtered and so people do not get ill as often. Once the well was completed Alemitu's mother gave her an exercise book so that she could start school.

ice lollies

Children collecting water in Ethiopia. Photo: Christian Aid

Activity Ideas

The children can act out Alemitu's story. They can try carrying heavy buckets of water and imagine what it must have been like for Alemitu. They can also make a list of the number of times they need water in a day. How much water do they use in a day? How many buckets would they need?

The group can then make Injera, an Ethiopian pancake. Injeras are usually made from teff which is a type of millet flour. They are eaten with a spicy sauce called wot. This imitation Injera is easy to make and can be shared by the group.

Ethiopian pancakes

Pancake Recipe

* Sift 130g flour with a pinch of salt and a teaspoon of baking powder.

* Stir in up to 320 ml of milk to make a very thick batter.

* Grease a frying pan (preferably heavy based) with oil and heat until hot.

* Pour on some of the mixture and spread.

* Cover the pan with a lid and allow to cook for about 2 minutes until bubbles have formed and the mixture is spongy.

* Transfer to a plate - do not cook the second side.

Banner Making

Give each group a sheet of white card, a garden cane and sticky tape. Ask them to make a banner which illustrates what they have learnt about a child's life in another country. Each banner should be headed with the country's name and information the group has found out about it.

A fourth banner for Britain can be made by the whole group. It can include the same information as the other banners. Each child can draw a picture of themselves to be stuck on one side of the banner to form a collage of faces. These banners can then form part of an offertory procession or display for a Christian Aid Week service.

St John the Baptist

Seventeenth-century icon of John the Baptist from the Icon museum in Recklinghausen

The figure of John the Baptist is prominent in the early narratives of the gospels. His ministry prefigures that of Christ. John was a fearless man of uncompromising beliefs, a prophet with a clear mission to prepare the way for Christ.

John was the son of Zechariah, a priest of the Temple, and of Elizabeth a relation of Mary the Mother of Jesus. The birth of John, like that of Jesus, is foretold by an angel (Luke 1.8-20) who instructed Zechariah that he should be called John. After the birth narrative (Luke 1.57-80) John's next appearance is on the banks of the River Jordan warning people to repent and be baptized (Matthew 3.1-12, Mark 1.2-8, Luke 3.1-21). His dress and diet of locusts and wild honey were reminiscent of the Old Testament prophets. Jesus' baptism by John is recorded in all the synoptic gospels, (Matthew 3.13-17, Luke 3.21-22, Mark 1.9-11). John's criticism of Herod Antipas for his marriage led to his imprisonment and subsequent beheading (Matthew 14.1-12, Mark 6.14-29, Luke 9. 7-9). According to the Jewish historian Josephus, John was imprisoned and killed at the fortress of Machaerus by the Dead Sea.

ACTIVITY IDEAS

Themes

The life of John the Baptist provides the teacher with an abundance of themes. Three are explored here - naming; John's place in salvation history; and repentance.

Timing

Each activity can take one to two sessions.

1. A Birthday Sampler

Discussion ideas

June 24 is the festival of the birth of John the Baptist. The story of the angel visiting Zechariah and telling him that his son should be called John shows the importance attached to naming people in the ancient world. The Bible is full of the special names given to people and their meaning: Jacob, Moses, Samson, Peter the Rock, Sons of Thunder, Jesus, Paul.

Read Luke 1. 8-20 in the group and discuss the questions with them.

Activity

The group can then make a John the Baptist sampler-type picture on a large sheet of paper. The illustration should include his parents' names, his own, the date of birth, the place of birth and drawings which represent the meaning of his name and his life.

Each child can then make their own 'sampler'. They can also include their own photograph and pictures of their parents and siblings if they wish. The design can be simple or elaborate. The purpose is that the children understand more about their own name and identity.

You will need
paper
card or frame
ruler
drawing materials
name book
portrait photographs
scissors
picture or example of a birth sampler

2. A John the Baptist Mural

Divide the group into five smaller groups. Give each group instructions for painting a picture of the scene they have been given. Speech bubbles (SB) can be used to incorporate the text given. The five completed scenes can be mounted in church or on a school wall to produce a mural which shows John the Baptist's place in salvation history.

a) John continued the prophetic tradition. He wore clothes reminiscent of Elijah (2 Kings 1.8). Like Isaiah he preached about the coming of the Messiah (Isa. 40.3). Ask the group to read these passages and then draw the two Old Testament prophets. They can use speech bubbles to convey the message of the prophets.

b) John calls people to repent and be baptised. Ask the group to read Matthew 3.4 to find out what John looked like. Then they can draw him baptising people in the River Jordan. (SB Matthew 3.2)

c) Jesus is baptised by John, and God affirms this. Ask the group to read Matthew 3.16-17 and then draw Jesus being baptised. (SB Matthew 3.17)

d) Peter baptises people. Ask the group to read Acts 2.38 and illustrate the text.

e) A modern baptism. Take the form of service for a baptism into the session or take the group to a baptism service so that they can see what happens today when people are baptised. The group can then draw a modern baptism.

You will need

5 large sheets of paper

drawing materials

Bibles

paint

sticky tape

3. Repentance of Sins

John preached that people needed to prepare for Jesus' coming by repenting of their sins. For children repentance is 'saying you are sorry' for something that they know is wrong. In the group discuss with the children what actions they often do which they know to be wrong. Can they change their ways? Christians believe that God forgives sin once people have repented. A simple activity to visually illustrate this is a turn around card.

Give each child a sheet of card. On one side they should draw or write about something that they have done wrong in the previous week. Then ask them to draw or write about what they should have done on the reverse of the card.

The cards can be Blu-Tacked onto a wall with the 'wrong side' facing. The teacher can then lead a prayer of repentance with the group. As a prayer is said the children can turn around their cards to show that the wrong is forgiven and a new right way is opened up.

You will need

card

drawing materials

Blu-Tack

St Peter

A Fisherman and Rock of the Church

JUNE **29**th JUNE

The Call of Peter and Andrew from a sixth-century mosaic at San Apollinare Nuovo, Ravenna

The feast of St Peter is on 29 June. We know from the New Testament that he was called Simon, a native of Bethsaida and brother of Andrew (John 1.40-43) and a fisherman (Matthew 4.18). Jesus gave him the name of Cephas (Peter) which means rock. After his confession at Caesarea Philippi (Matthew 16.13-20) Jesus says to him, "You are Peter and on this rock I will build my church, and the powers of death shall not prevail against it. I will give you the keys of the kingdom of heaven," (RSV).

St Peter is often illustrated in Christian art holding a set of keys. After Jesus' death Peter retains a prominent position in the early Church. Early tradition maintains that he was martyred in Rome, crucified head downwards and was buried in the city.

ACTIVITY IDEAS

Themes

St Peter's day usually falls just before the school holidays. Many Sunday schools are coming to a close around this time too. These activities are therefore designed to be suitable for holiday groups or for children going on holiday. They aim to help the children understand more about the life of a fisherman on the Sea of Galilee. They also explore some of the imagery associated with St Peter.

Resources

If possible go on a seaside walk with the children before St Peter's day to collect shells, pebbles and seaweed or ask them to bring in holiday mementos or books on the seaside and fishing.

Timing

Each activity will take one to two sessions.

DISCUSSION QUESTIONS
* What qualities does a rock have?
* Can they think of another story in the New Testament where rock is mentioned? (see Matthew 7. 24-27)
* What qualities did St Peter need to build up a church?
* When was Peter strong?
* When did he let Jesus down?
* Can they think of other Christians they could call a rock?

1. "On this rock I will build my church"

Discuss with the children why Peter was called a rock using these questions.

Pebble Painting

The children can draw symbols of St Peter (fishing net, keys, fish or a ship), his name, or a picture of their church or a symbol of a church on pebbles. Younger children can try using chalks. Older ones might use paint and varnish the finished result.

You will need

smooth pebbles

chalks

paints

varnish

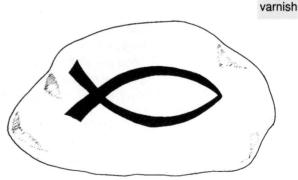

2. Living by the Sea of Galilee

Drama

Read the following Bible passages with the group. What do they say about the life of a fisherman at the time of Jesus?

Mark 1.16-20 The call of the disciples

Mark 4.35-41 Stilling the storm

Ask the children to read the story of the miraculous catch of fish aloud (Luke 5.1-11) and encourage them to act it out.

St Peter's Fish

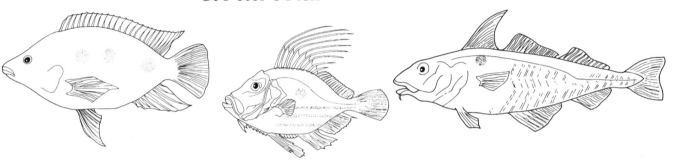

St Peter's fish: Tilapia, John Dory and Haddock

"Go to the sea and cast a hook, and take the first fish that comes up, and when you open its mouth you will find a shekel; take that and give it to them for me and for yourself." (Matthew 17.27)

This account of Jesus' response to Peter about paying the Temple tribute money has led to a wide variety of fish being named after the saint. Traditionally the haddock was believed to be the fish and the two marks on the fish's neck are said to be the impressions of the finger and thumb of the Apostle as he held the fish to take out the shekel. The oval black spots on a John Dory fish are also said to be the Apostle's finger-marks and this fish is known in Europe as St Peter's Fish. In fact the most likely contender to be the original St Peter's fish is the tilapia. Tilapia flourish in fresh water and the way they nurture their young throws some light on the biblical story. They carry their eggs and later the young fish within their mouths. When the parent fish wishes to keep out her young it will pick up an object (a bright one, preferably) and keep it in her mouth to prevent their return. The coin in the fish's mouth in the biblical story could have been such a bright object.

The group can copy the fish illustrated here to create their own St Peter's fish design using brightly coloured collage or colouring materials. Older children could model the fish in salt dough and paint them.

You will need

copies of fish

paper

colouring materials

shiny paper

scissors

glue

salt dough

The Sea of Galilee

Discuss with the group what they might see if they looked down into the Sea of Galilee. Each child can then make their own Sea of Galilee model.

* Cut the centre out of one of the plates.

* With the rim of the plate right side up, glue clear plastic across the opening to create a window.

* Cut out fish shapes (perhaps St Peter's fish with a shekel in its mouth) from the discarded centre section of the plate. Decorate them.

* Colour the uncut plate centre blue.

* Glue fish, wool 'seaweed', pebbles, sand and pasta shapes to create a sea effect on the uncut plate.

* Cover this with the upside down cut plate and staple the two plates together.

* Decorate the outside of the sea picture on the rim of the plate. A walnut half could become a boat and be stuck to the rim of the scene.

You will need

two paper plates for each child

scissors and PVA glue

wool scraps

felt pens

stapler

clear plastic wrap

coloured cellophane or sweet wrappers

sand, pebbles, shells, pasta shapes

walnut halves (optional)

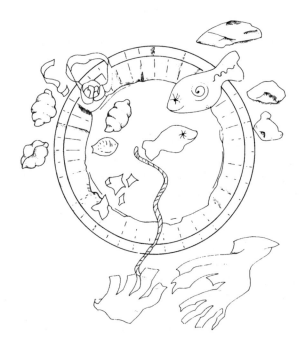

Paper plate sea scenes

St Aidan of Lindisfarne

St Aidan and the Celtic Tradition

St Aidan. Tapestry in The Chapel of English Saints, Gloucester Cathedral. Photo: RJL Smith, Much Wenlock

St Aidan lived in the seventh century. Like King Oswald, who was king of Northumbria, Aidan was educated in Iona in Scotland. Oswald wanted his subjects to share his Christian faith so he called upon the monastic community at Iona to supply him with a missionary. Aidan was sent. Oswald gave him as his see the small island of Lindisfarne on the Northumbrian coast near today's Berwick-upon-Tweed.

The stories of Aidan and the other Northumbrian saints recorded in Bede's *A History of the English Church and People* have retained their rich vividness through the centuries. Bede records that Aidan was an "inspiring example of self-discipline and continence" to his clergy. "He never sought or cared for any worldly possession, and loved to give away to the poor whatever he received from kings or wealthy folk." Aidan travelled everywhere on foot speaking to everyone he met on the way. If they were pagan he urged them to be baptised. All who went with him were required to meditate and read the scriptures.

He was also a man of uncompromising beliefs. If asked to dine with the king, he would eat sparingly and leave as soon as possible in order to pray. We are told he sometimes went to pray in solitude on Farne island. "If wealthy people did wrong, he never kept silent out of respect for their position, but corrected them outspokenly". Money given to him by the rich was given to the poor or used to ransom slaves. Bede tells the story that King Oswin gave Bishop Aidan a fine horse for his work. When a poor man asked Aidan for alms the Bishop dismounted and gave the beggar the horse. When King Oswin questioned Aidan about giving away such a valuable horse to a beggar the Bishop replied:"What are you saying, Your Majesty? Is this foal of a mare more valuable to you than the Son of God?"

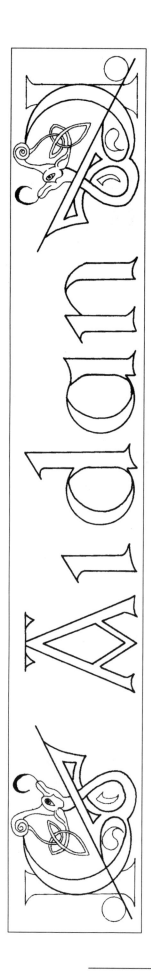

Aidan's influence was widespread. The monasteries and schools he set up helped nurture the church in Northumbria at a time when it was the greatest of the Anglo-Saxon kingdoms. Most of the North and Midlands were evangelised by monks and nuns who owed their allegiance to Lindisfarne including Wilfrid, Cuthbert, Cedd, Cynebil, Caelin, Chad, Hilda of Whitby and Ebbe of Coldingham.

ACTIVITY IDEAS

Themes

The stories about St Aidan and his followers provide a rich introduction to Celtic spirituality for children. This is explored in the first activity. The second activity helps children appreciate the artistry of the Lindisfarne Gospels.

Resources

Further information is available from the Marygate Community on Holy Island who produce a lively series of illustrated leaflets on the saints of Lindisfarne. Contact Marygate House, Holy Island Berwick-upon-Tweed. TD15 25D. The Lindisfarne Gospels can be viewed in the British Library.

Timing

Allow two sessions for these activities.

1. Celtic Spirituality

When the Celts became Christian they retained a spirituality that celebrated God in nature and in the everyday. Every aspect of daily life was invested with religious significance. God was not distant, he was immanent. Aidan shared this spirituality. His lifestyle was simple, his message direct. On his walking missions he preached to all he met wherever and whoever they were. The aim of the walking activity is to help children experience something of Aidan's simplicity and spirituality and to see how prayer is integral to all that they do.

A prayer walk

At the beginning of the session explain that they are going to go on a walk like St Aidan. Like him they will greet and meet people and understand more about the immediate neighbourhood. Ask the children to pray about what they are doing and those they will meet, asking for God's blessing. The walk can be a short circuit around the immediate area or it can take in a longer route ending with pre-arranged refreshments at a parishioner's house. This activity can be adapted to suit the local situation. The walk might provide an opportunity for the group to visit a local retirement home, or for the children to post Baptism Anniversary cards or Harvest invitations around the parish. Some children might want to take token cards or gifts they have made.

You will need

paper and drawing materials

adequate adult supervision for the walk

refreshments

materials for invitations, home-made biscuits or flowers

After the walk, talk with the children about what they saw, what happened and who they met.

Younger children can record their experience by captioning their drawings of the walk with short prayers. eg "We met Mrs Brown who is ill. Please Lord help her to get better." The drawings can be:

* a large picture map of the people and places they saw
* a frieze of the whole of their walk
* a loose-leaf album of drawings from all the children

Older children can share their experiences of the walk with each other. Encourage them to share these feelings in prayer.

2. The Lindisfarne Gospels

Forty-seven years after Aidan's death a monk at Lindisfarne called Eadfrith set himself the task of writing the four gospels in Latin - the Lindisfarne Gospels. The gospels are brilliant examples of the Celtic art of the time. Each page was painstakingly pricked out, the Latin text written and the whole page beautifully decorated. The lettering was done with pens made from goose quills or reeds. These manuscripts were written to glorify God and remain a living testament to the spirituality and artistry of the Lindisfarne monks.

Celtic lettering

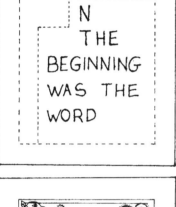

Younger children can colour in copies of the AIDAN lettering. Suggest that they draw their own animals around the letters. Can they write their own name with letters like this?

An illuminated page

Older children can make their own quills with careful supervision. They should use feathers, preferably goose feathers, and cut out the points as shown.

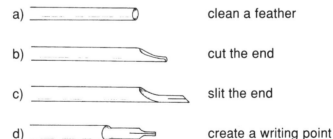

a)   clean a feather

b)   cut the end

c)   slit the end

d)   create a writing point

After they have looked at copies of the illuminated page they can experiment and create an illuminated page based on their own initial, using the quills they have made and coloured inks. Some groups might prefer to do an illuminated page using felt pens.

You will need

copies of the illuminated manuscript shown here

copies of AIDAN lettering

drawing materials

feathers

Stanley knife

inks

Harvest

A Celebration of Thanksgiving

The harvest celebration of today continues a tradition of thanksgiving which was an essential part of the worship of Israel from earliest times. Jews and Christians give thanks to God for the abundance of his creation. The first fruits of the harvest were considered of particular importance. In Britain worshippers would take the first ripe corn to church in August and bread made from this corn was offered at the communion. This gave us the name of the season, Lammas or loaf-mass, which survives to this day in some areas.

The more common autumn festival at the end of harvest which we know today began only 150 years ago in Cornwall. The Revd R.S. Hawker of Morwenstow asked his parishioners to come to church on the first Sunday in October to thank God for the good harvest. The traditional harvest home, the feast enjoyed by farm workers when the corn was gathered in, was also influenced by the Church in the middle of the last century.

Harvest is an adaptable festival. In this century churches have often focused on harvests other than the agricultural. In fishing ports they might celebrate the harvest of the sea; in industrial areas the harvest of industry. Harvest can also be a time to remember people's labour and talents.

From the earliest Jewish tradition harvest was a time to remember the poor and those in need. Leviticus 19 encourages farmers who have harvested their crop not to go back to the edges of their field to collect any remaining corn as this should be left for the poor and foreigners. This concern for the poor appears again in the New Testament (2 Corinthians 9.6-15).

Today many churches use harvest time to focus on people in the Two-Thirds World who cannot rely on good harvests, or on the poor in their own community. The concern for ecology in the 1980s and 1990s has led to an increased emphasis at harvest time on our stewardship of God's earth.

ACTIVITY IDEAS

Themes

Whatever the local emphasis of the harvest festival its themes are constant - God's gifts; thanksgiving; celebration; and concern for others. These themes are explored here using Psalm 65 as a starting point.

Timing

All these activities can form part of a special harvest service. Activity 1 needs advance planning and should be prepared the week before harvest. It takes 1 session. The two alternatives given in Activity 2 could take a session each.

1. Crowning the Year

> "You crown the year with your bounty,
> abundance flows wherever you pass;
> the desert pastures overflow,
> the hillsides are wrapped in joy,
> the meadows are dressed in flocks,
> the valleys are clothed in wheat,
> what shouts of joy, what singing!"
> *(Psalm 65.11-13 : The Jerusalem Bible)*

The Jewish people of the Old Testament believed that the seasons, weather and harvest were controlled by God. In Psalm 65 the blessing of the fertility of the earth is seen as God crowning the year. Inspired by the abundance of the fruits of the earth the Psalmist imagines the year as a queen that has been crowned by God himself with divine jewels and bounty. This imagery of crowning is a rich one to explore with children.

On the Sunday before the harvest festival read Psalm 65 to the children. Ask them, Who wears a crown? Why is a crown precious? In what way could a crown show the richness of the fruits of the earth? etc.

Then the children can make their own crowns. These can be a simple foil pie dish with a cardboard coronet attached or it could be a more elaborate and decorated crown.

These crowns can serve two purposes. They can be a teaching aid to show the richness of God's creation and they can be used as a container for a harvest gift for a housebound person.

If the crowns are to be used purely as a teaching aid then the children can be encouraged to take home their crowns and fill them with something which shows the variety and richness of God's creation. They could collect different leaves to illustrate the variety of trees, or flowers, or shells etc.

If the crowns are also to be used as containers for harvest gifts ask the children to consider a suitable present for a housebound person which could also show the wealth of God's creation. The crowns could be filled with fruits, sweets and cakes. Ask the group to take their crowns home and to fill them for the following Sunday.

At the harvest festival the filled crowns can be taken up during the offertory and given as a symbol of thanks for God's goodness.

You will need

foil pie plates

cardboard strips

scissors

stapler

drawing materials

decorative materials

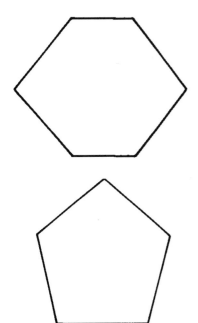

2. Giving Thanks for God's Blessings

Jewels in the crown

This activity is designed so that children can look at their own lives and give thanks for the gifts that God has given them through the year.

Discuss with the children what have been the special occasions and achievements of the past year - things they have done at school, family celebrations, special occasions in the community etc. What have they received that they can give thanks to God for? The jewel templates can symbolise the richness of God's blessings.

Give each child a number of jewel templates. In each of these shapes they should draw or write about the special blessings they have received in the previous year. Each of these jewels can be put in the crown and taken up during the offertory procession.

You will need

a crown from activity 1

copies of the jewel templates on coloured paper

drawing materials

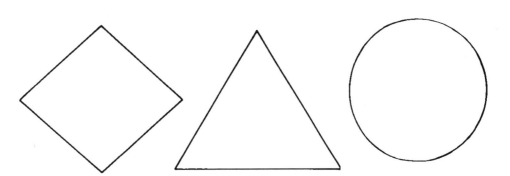

A thanksgiving song

Ask the younger children to look out of the window or go outside and tell their teacher what things they can see.

The older children can be given a task of making a list of 10 things, with the aim of finding things which no-one else in the group sees.

Once the group comes together again get them to make a list on a large sheet of paper of the things they have seen. Ask them to say what is good about each item. e.g. The trees give us shade on a hot day. The flowers are colourful. The cans can be recycled etc. Then ask the children to link these phrases together using the response - "We thank you God for your gifts."

The children could set this Psalm-like song to music or a beat, or it could be read out during a harvest service.

St Francis of Assisi

A Saint for All Ages

Stained glass window at the Church of Reconciliation at Taizé, France

Few saints have inspired such affection and loyalty as St Francis. His popularity has lasted centuries and his appeal is as attractive to children and adults today as it was nearly 800 years ago.

Francis was born into a rich merchant's family in Assisi in 1182 and until he was twenty he worked for his father in the family's cloth business. Francis enjoyed life and was known in the town as gallant and high spirited. During a long illness Francis decided to devote himself to prayer and service of the poor. On a pilgrimage to Rome he exchanged his clothes with those of a beggar and spent the rest of the day begging himself. This experience had a profound effect on him and his attitude to poverty.

When he returned to Assisi, Francis devoted his time to caring for lepers and repairing the ruined church of S. Damiano. One morning while praying in the church of Portiuncula he heard the commission of Christ to the twelve disciples. Francis understood this to be directed to him personally and he left his staff and shoes and put on a long dark garment girded with a cord and began his new mission. The simplicity of his message and call to poverty attracted many followers. Francis drew up a simple rule of life for himself and his friends, the *Regula Primitiva*, based on the sayings from the Gospels.

The followers of St Francis became known as the friars minor. In 1212 Francis's ideas were accepted by Clare, a lady of Assisi, who founded a similar society for women centred on the church of S. Damiano. This Second Order of Franciscans of Contemplative nuns became known as Poor Clares. In 1221 Francis founded the Tertiaries, a group of people who lived in the world and wanted to adopt his ideals as far as was compatible with everyday life.

Francis died on 3 October 1226 and he was canonized two years later by Pope Gregory IX. His feast day is 4 October.

ACTIVITY IDEAS

Themes

St Francis can be the starting point for a number of themes - love of animals, life-style, religious orders, concern for the poor etc. The activities given here concentrate on what St Francis teaches us about care for the earth and a rule of life.

Resources

There are plenty of suitable books on the life of St Francis for older children. *Stories of St Francis* (Glow-worm Books/ Mowbrays) is suitable for younger children. *Growing - a Parish Youth Programme* by Susan Sayers (Kevin Mayhew Ltd) includes the text and music of a musical play based on the life of St Francis.

Timing

These activities take one to two sessions.

1. The Canticle of the Sun

St Francis regarded the whole of God's creation as part of his family. He called the sun, 'brother sun' and the water, 'sister water'. The hymn of praise he composed at the end of his life, called the *Canticle of the Sun*, can be found in most hymn books as "All Creatures of Our God and King". The session could include singing this hymn with the children.

Invite the children to think about all the birds, animals, trees, flowers, fruits, insects, fish etc in God's creation and choose one they would like to have as their 'brother' or 'sister'. Ask them to explain their choice. Get them to think about what it means if something in creation is my 'brother' or 'sister' - that we must love and care and be concerned for it.

The activity suggestions are designed to get the group to think about the stewardship of God's earth and its conservation.

Bird feeders (for younger children)

This activity is a practical way for younger children to explore the idea of a 'brother' or 'sister' bird that they care for.

The group can make their own bird feeders:

* Take 3 net bags from fruit or onions (one net bag inside another reduces the size of the holes)

* Fill separate bags with peanuts, maize and sunflower seeds.

You will need

net bags

peanuts

maize

sunflower seeds

string

plastic saucers

* Tie them together.

* Tie string to the top of the bag.

* Make a hole in the top of the plastic saucer.

* Thread the string from the top of the feeder through the upturned saucer and attach to a tree. The saucer protects the food from rain.

Another way of making a feeder is to take of mixture of seeds and dried fruit and stir in melted dripping. Put this mixture into a yogurt pot mould and set in the fridge. The yogurt pot should have a string threaded through the top so that it can be hung up.

The life in an oak tree (for older children)

A simple way for the group to appreciate the variety and beauty of creation is for them to create a collage of all the animals, birds and insects that live on an oak tree. If possible look at a real tree with the group and collect fallen oak leaves and acorns.

* Paint a large trunk of the tree from paper and card.

* Oak leaves can be made from making leaf prints with paint or by making a wax crayon rubbing of a leaf. Stick these on the tree. Some leaves could be partly stuck down to reveal an insect or animal underneath.

* Make the animals and insects out of collage materials or paper and add to the tree.

You will need

paper

drawing materials

collage materials

glue

paint

oak leaves

2. A Way of Life

St Francis chose to live in poverty. Remind the children how he sold a bale of his father's best silk and gave the money to a priest to repair a ruined church. Francis's father was furious and took him to the market place where he reprimanded him for stealing from him when he had always given Francis whatever he wanted. Francis took off all his clothes and gave them back to his father saying, "Here are the clothes you have given me. From now on, I will obey only my Father in Heaven."

Discuss this story with the children and point out that Francis chose to live without fine clothes and all the things he wanted. Ask them to make a list of the things they would like for their next birthday or Christmas. Then ask them to cross out all those things they could live without. It is a demanding and difficult thing to do.

Franciscans live by a rule of life. Some of the children will be familiar with the Brownie or Cub Promise and be able to explain it. Remind them that a rule does not have to be a lot of 'don'ts' but a statement of what 'I intend to be'. Look at what St Francis said to his father and the prayer of St Francis *(Make me a channel of your peace)* with the children. Divide the group into pairs and ask them to decide on three statements of 'What I intend to be' which they could write on a special card. Suggest that they put these cards in their bedroom and try to follow their own 'rule of life'.

One World Week

*Children from Melrose Grammar
School in a Shanty Town they
built for One World Week*

One World Week is an annual DIY education and action week, focusing on the issues of justice, peace, development and the environment. One World Week originated in 1978 as an experiment by the Churches' Committee of the World Development Movement. The experiment was a success and the week is now an established festival in many churches, schools and groups. It is ecumenical. It is local. There is no fund-raising campaign, nor a centralised initiative. This is an occasion for celebration, study and participation by everyone.

Each year the One World Week office provides the general theme, a study/action guide and publicity material. While the theme is different each year, the overriding aim is the same - to open doors so that people see that they are part of a bigger world than they may have thought.

ACTIVITY IDEAS

Themes

The aim of One World Week is to get local groups to work out their own plans on the annual theme. These suggestions can provide a starting point for groups. The activities help groups understand more about the world in which we live.

Resources

One World Week, P.O. Box 100, London SEI 7RT. Tel. 071-620 4444

World Aware (The Centre for World Development Education), 1 Catton Street, London WCIR 4AB, produces a catalogue of resources in development education.

The National Association for Development Education Centres, 6 Endsleigh St, London WC1H ODX, has a list of all the local development education centres.

Contact your local diocesan development representative.

Timing

The activities listed in 1. can take anything from 10 minutes to 30 minutes. The second activity requires more planning and at least a 30 minute session.

1. Learning about the World

The aim of these activities is to help children understand more about the geography of the world. The games are designed so that the children have to work as a team and co-operate together. The games also provide a useful resource for other games.

A jigsaw map

Younger children might not be familiar with the geography of the world. Before the session prepare an outline map of the world traced from an atlas. Enlarge this by photocopying and stick onto a piece of card. Cut this out into different shapes. This can then be the resource for group activity games on fitting the world together. The children need to work together referring to a picture of the world to complete their jigsaw.

You will need

a globe

a football

an atlas

thin paper

card

scissors

glue

drawing materials

Where on earth?

* draw country maps on graph paper hiding the names of the capital cities in a word-grid.

* make an anagram quiz of the names of countries and capitals.

* take everyday commodities from the larder and ask the children where our food comes from.

* get the children to bring in foods from different countries.

* find out about the traditional food from different countries and have an international meal.

* get the children to bring in leaves from trees and shrubs and help them find out where they originate from.

Older children can work on a globe figure. Before the session carefully wet thin paper and press onto the globe. Trace around the countries or continents, wait for the paper to dry and then cut out the shapes. Take the globe, or a football, and the mixed up shapes to the session. Then get the children to put the shapes in place.

2. Experiencing Injustice in the World - The Human Race Game

This game needs to be adapted to suit local conditions. It is suitable for groups of at least 8 children aged between 7 and 14. The purpose of the game is to help children appreciate the injustices faced by the majority of the human race, whether they are handicapped or financially poor. In advance of the session set out three main areas in the room and have an adult supervising each area. The food store - where there are two plates of good food and two plates of bread. The toilet facilities - where two children are able to wash in a sink and go to the toilet while the others are faced with two bowls of water containing plastic insects. The sleeping area - with two Z-beds with sleeping bags, two mats, newspapers and boxes.

Before the game starts. Put one child in a wheelchair, blindfold one, ask one child to hop and a pair of children to piggy back around the game.

Then explain to the children that they are children from different countries. In this game they have to get themselves a meal, wash and then go to bed, in that order. Explain that it is a cold night. Give the two able-bodied children three tokens each. Many children believe it to be a competitive race.

When the children arrive at the food table, only those who can buy a meal with one token are given the good food. The others get the bread on a first-come, first-served basis after the others have eaten some of their feasts. At the toilet facilities only those with a token are able to use the good facilities. The others have to wait until those with tokens have washed and then they use the bowls with insects in. At the sleeping facilities the Z-beds cost one token and the others have to make do with what is available. Once all the children have been round the course let them come together for a discussion.

You will need

(for a group of 8 children)

large room or garden

toilet facilities

2 plates of good food

2 plates of bread

6 tokens

2 bowls of water with plastic insects in

2 Z-beds with sleeping bags

2 mats

cardboard boxes and newspaper

a blindfold

a wheelchair (if space)

Ask the children:

How they feel about the race?

What were the experiences of those who were handicapped?

Who would they have preferred to be in the race?

What are the consequences of always eating poor food or having poor washing facilities?

What part of the world do the children think they are from?

Did any of them share their facilities or tokens?

Did some of them think it was a race?

Ask them what parallels can be drawn between their lives and real life in Britain and elsewhere.

All Saints

Celebrating the Heroes of the Faith

Mother Teresa of Calcutta and Archbishop Desmond Tutu. St Mark's Church, Altadena, USA. Photo: Virginia Merrill, The Episcopal News

Children today are more likely to know about Hallowe'en rather than All Saints. In Europe the Christian festivals of All Saints on 1 November and All Souls on 2 November coincided with the festivals of the ancient Celtic New Year, Samhain. Another name for All Saints' Day is All Hallows, and the day before is All Hallows Eve, or Hallowe'en. Often customs practised on Hallowe'en owe their origin to pre-Christian rather than Christian traditions, and throughout Church history there has been a tension between the two. Many Christians are disturbed by the increase of interest in the pre-Christian aspects of Hallowe'en. One way to counteract this at a local level is to make All Saints' Tide once again a great Christian celebration of faith. In addition All Saints provides an excellent excuse for a great church party.

ACTIVITY IDEAS

Themes

The ASB collect for All Saints' Day draws together the themes of the season. The heroes of the faith provide us with models of the Christian life. This is a time to give thanks to God for such shining examples of the faith. All Saints can be an occasion to remember those saints who have no special commemoration in the Christian year. It can also be the time to remember the modern heroes of the faith. Modern day saints may be those who have fought against disease, ignorance, poverty or injustice.

In the New Testament "saints" often means Christians in general, Romans 1.7, 1 Corinthians 1.2, Ephesians 2.19. All Saints is the time of year to remember that all Christians are united in a communion of faith.

The activities explore these themes. They aim to show how all saints are united in a Christian family and how each child is part of that family. The activities can also form part of an All Saints party or church celebration.

Resources

Useful books on modern saints include:

Faith in Action series (RMEP)

People with a Purpose series (SCM)

Timing

One to two sessions.

Group discussion

Discuss with the group what they understand by saints.

Then read out the Collect for All Saints with the children. Remind them that all Christians are saints - we are all called to be shining examples of the Christian life. Christians are 'knitted together' as a family of believers. Some like St Francis, St Nicholas, St Peter and St Joan lived hundreds of years ago. Other, modern heroes of the faith, like Martin Luther King, Desmond Tutu, Oscar Romero and Jackie Pullinger have had great influence on the modern church. Remind the group that they are part of this Christian family, this communion of saints. Through their belief and Christian life they are united with the hundreds of men and women who have followed Christ through the ages and throughout the world.

PRAYER

Almighty God,

you have knit together your elect

into one communion and fellowship

in the mystical body of your Son.

Give us grace so to follow your blessed saints

in all virtuous and godly living,

that we may come to those unspeakable joys

which you have prepared for those who truly love you;

through Jesus Christ our Lord.

(ASB collect for All Saints' Day)

DISCUSSION QUESTIONS

* Who are saints?

* What do they do?

* Are there saints today?

* Who are they?

1. A Chain of Saints

* Cut a long strip from a large sheet of paper.

* Concertina the paper into four.

* Ask the children to draw and then cut out a figure making sure both hands are part of the fold. See illustration.

* Unfold to reveal a chain of figures.

* The younger children can then draw on each of the figures. The first saint can be of their church dedication. The second of a saint they particularly like. The third of someone they know who is a good example of the Christian life and the fourth a picture of themselves.

* The children might want to add tissue paper clothes to the figures.

These chains can form a frieze, they can be stood around church candlesticks or they can decorate a church room for a party. Alternatively they can be used to make an All Saints lantern.

You will need

paper

drawing materials

scissors

glue

glass jars

string

candles

matches

tapers

tissue paper

Blu-Tack

2. An All Saints Lantern

* Glue the chain around a clean, clear jam jar, overlapping if necessary.

* In the jar place a small night light. Secure the base with Blu-Tack.

* Attach string around the neck of the jar and make a handle.

* These completed lanterns can be lit with a taper for an All Saints procession or be a table decoration at an All Saints party.

3. All Saints Flags

* Give each child a plain flag shape.

* Ask them to draw a picture of their favourite saint on one side and a picture of themselves on the other.

* Attach to a pea stick with glue.

* These can be used in a party, a procession or a special All Saints dance.

You will need

pea sticks

ready-made flag shapes

glue

drawing materials

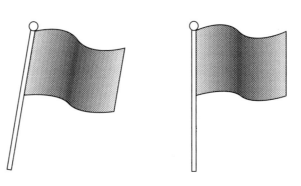

4. A Woven Banner

This All Saints banner shows how all Christians are knitted together in God's family. The whole group needs to work together for this activity.

* Tie the lengths of wool to the top and bottom canes to make the warp threads.

* Connect a loop of wool to the top cane to make the hanger.

* Hang the banner up and get the group to weave the different colours of material strips through the wool. Neaten the ends by tying them together. This creates a woven-type banner.

* Each colour of sugar paper can represent different people. Make cut-out figures as instructed in activity 1. These can then be woven (tucked) into the banner to create a 'communion of saints'.

* Put one figure representing Jesus at the top.

* Under this put eleven figures to represent the disciples.

* The next line is the people who founded our church - saints, church patrons etc.

* The last row of figures represents the group themselves.

You will need

two large canes

thick string/wool cut into the lengths of the banner plus 10cm

strips of material, tights, ribbons, plastic sheeting and paper the width of the banner or one piece of cloth to make the banner

four colours of sugar paper

drawing materials

scissors

St Cecilia

Patron Saint of Music

NOVEMBER · 22nd · NOVEMBER

Detail from window by Burne-Jones at Christ Church Cathedral, Oxford. Photo: Woodmansterne (Jeremy Marks)

St Cecilia is one of those saints whose fame extends far beyond the Church and whose memory is widely treasured. She probably lived in the second or third century and was buried in Rome. Little more than this is actually known about her.

The popularity of St Cecilia is largely due to a late fifth-century legend. This said she was a young Christian patrician, betrothed to a pagan called Valerian. As she had already vowed her virginity to God she refused to consummate the marriage. Both her husband and his brother, Tiburtius, became Christians and were martyred. Later Cecilia herself was also martyred.

This story is not substantiated by any reliable contemporary evidence but the fascination of her character has inspired many literary works and many songs. Her patronage of music is said to date from a verse from her legend: "As the organs (at her wedding feast) were playing, Cecilia sung (in her heart) to the Lord, saying, 'May my heart remain unsullied, so that I be not confounded'."

St Cecilia is the patron of church music, organists and the blind and is frequently represented in art playing the organ. Her feast day is on 22 November.

ACTIVITY IDEAS

Themes

Although St Cecilia does not appear in the ASB calendar her feast day provides an opportunity to explore music in worship with children.

Resources

There are many books on making musical instruments which could be used to augment the suggestions given here. Particularly useful is *Junk Instruments - How to Make and Play Them* by Andy Jackson (Red Fox).

Timing

Activities 1 and 2 can be done in one or two sessions. Activity 3 forms a logical continuation of the first two but can be carried out in a separate session. The activities could also provide the basis for a St Cecilia's Day service.

1. Praising God through the Psalms

PSALM 150

Alleluia!

Praise God in his Temple on earth,

praise him in his temple in heaven,

praise him for his mighty achievements,

praise him for his transcendent greatness!

Praise him with blasts of the trumpet,

praise him with lyre and harp,

praise him with drums and dancing,

praise him with strings and reeds,

praise him with clashing cymbals,

praise him with clanging cymbals!

Let everything that breathes praise Yahweh!

Alleluia!

(Jerusalem Bible)

In the Old Testament the Psalms provide a rich source of material about the worship of God's people. One way the Psalms can be brought alive for children is to get them to perform with their own instruments the Psalmist's hymns of praise. Start with Psalm 150 - the Great Alleluia Psalm.

Few Psalms or hymns equal the exuberance of praise of Psalm 150. It begins and ends with Alleluia which means Praise the Lord. The Psalmist clearly indicates what musical instruments are needed and it is likely that this Psalm was part of a festival liturgy of the Temple worship. There are eight instruments mentioned and these roughly fall into three categories: string instruments, wind instruments and percussion. Children can make their own instruments and use them to perform the Psalm themselves. Divide the group into three and give each group one category of instruments to make.

Once the instruments have been made they can be used as an accompaniment to the Psalm. As each instrument is mentioned in the Psalm the children can play the most appropriate instrument they have made. Alternatively the instruments could be used to accompany one of the many settings of Psalm 150.

2. Making Instruments

String Instruments - a biscuit tin harp

A simple box harp can be made from stretching different sizes and thicknesses of elastic bands around a biscuit tin.

Wind instruments - a hose trumpet

Many children will be familiar with tin whistles, recorders and even comb and paper.

They can improvise a trumpet by taking the rubber tap connection from a shower attachment. By blowing a

You will need

different sized elastic bands

biscuit tin

rubber shower attachment and funnel shape

pan lids

card

scissors

Blu-Tack

tape

10-pence coins

saucepans, bowls, flowerpots

thick plastic

beaters

Bibles

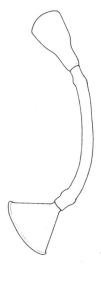

raspberry down the tube you can get a trumpet sound. This sound can be modified by adding a funnel shape at the end of the tube.

Percussion - cymbals and drums

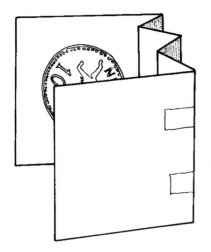

Cymbals feature prominently in Psalm 150. Large cymbals can be improvised using pan lids.

Simple hand cymbals or castanets can be made from a piece of card and two 10-pence coins. On a strip of card score a straight line down the centre. Reverse the card and score two lines, 1cm either side of the centre. On the original side score a further two lines 2cm from the centre line. Concertina the card as shown in the diagram. Secure the back of the folded card with tape so that the flaps spring apart. Using Blu-Tack, fix the two 10-pence pieces facing each other inside the flaps. The cymbals can then by played with one hand.

Drums were widely used in Old Testament times. Drums can be made from saucepans, pudding or mixing bowls, or large flower pots covered with thick plastic to form a tight membrane. These can be beaten with a stick or wooden spoon.

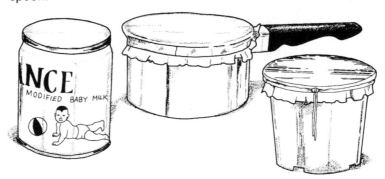

3. Songs of Praise

Children can be encouraged to create their own songs of praise to God. This can be done in a number of ways:

* by composing a poem that they set to music.

* by composing a rap after clapping the rhythm of their poem.

* by creating a simple song or round on the word Alleluia.

* by exploring further the Psalmist's language of praise.

Ask the children to look up the following verses about singing in the Psalms - 9:1-2; 33:3; 92:1,2,4; 95:1; 147:1,7; 148:13. Then divide the children into two groups. The first group should ask the question "What shall I sing to you God?" and the second group can reply with a verse from the Psalms listed. This can be continued through the verses to create a great antiphonal shout of praise.

St Andrew

Patron Saint of Scotland

NOVEMBER 30th NOVEMBER

Bronze of St Andrew the Fisherman in Grey Coat Hospital School, by Bernard Merry

The festival of St Andrew on 30 November is traditionally a time when the Anglican church pays special attention to its mission. St Andrew brought Peter to Jesus (John 1.35-42) and so was one of the first missionaries.

From the New Testament we learn that Andrew was Simon Peter's brother (Mark 1.16), a native of Bethsaida (John 1.44) who lived in Capernaum (Mark 1.29), and a fisherman (Matthew 4.18-20) who had been a follower of John the Baptist before he followed Jesus (John 1.35-40). Special mention is made of Andrew in the miracle of the feeding of the multitude where he finds the boy with the five loaves of bread and two fish (John 6.8ff), and in the episode of the Greeks who wished to meet Jesus (John 12.20-22).

From around AD 750 St Andrew has been the patron saint of Scotland. The legend is that St Rule, a native of Patras, was told by an angel to take the relics of St Andrew to an unknown destination in the north west. The saint travelled until the angel told him to stop. Here he built a church to house the relics and the town later became known as St Andrews.

One legend says that Andrew was crucified at Patras. The Apostle acknowledged that he was not worthy to die as Jesus had died and so elected to be crucified on a Greek X-shaped (saltire) cross. This cross became his symbol. In the Scottish flag it appears as a white cross (for St Andrew's purity) on a blue background (representing the sea) and this forms part of the Union Jack. His other symbol is a fishing-net reflecting his patronage of fishermen and sailors.

ACTIVITY IDEAS

Themes

These activities explore the mission of the church and remember those agencies and people committed to mission work. They also aim to help groups learn more about the Anglican church. Teachers should adapt the activities to suit their local situation.

Resources

Most of the mission societies have suitable teaching materials to supplement this chapter.

Timing

Each activity takes one session.

1. A Church Network Poster

The week before St Andrew's day ask the group to find out where they have links with other churches. This could include the place where their parents were married, where members of their family worship or where a relative was buried. Ask them to bring in pictures of these people or places if possible.

The following week discuss with the group all the places and people the church has links with - through families, mission societies, holiday churches, etc. The 'extended church family' is like a large fishing net linking people of many cultures and traditions together. This can be illustrated visually by making a church network poster.

* Ask the group to put photographs or draw pictures of themselves in the centre of the paper.

* Around this they can glue photographs or draw pictures of all the places and people they have links with.

* Ask each child to link their portrait picture with the other pictures they have links with. They should do this with pins and thread.

* Some children will have the same links, some will have different ones. The end result should be a large 'net' of people and places.

* A heading such as *Our Extended Church Family* or *Our Church's Network* can be added to the picture.

* To create a St Andrewstide border for the poster younger children can do potato prints in blue paint of the St Andrew's cross. Older children or the teacher will need to prepare the potatoes in advance by gouging out a x- shape in a potato half.

St Andrew's crosses

You will need

photographs and pictures from the children

mission society materials

large sheet of paper

thread

pins

potatoes

blue paint

knives

drawing materials

scissors

2. A Compasrose Mobile

The emblem of the worldwide Anglican Church, the Anglican Communion, is the compasrose. The symbol is used throughout the Anglican world. The centre of the emblem is the red cross of St George on a silver shield. This serves as a reminder of the English origins of the Anglican Communion. Encircling the cross is a band with the Greek inscription - "The truth shall make you free". From this band radiate all the points of the compass, symbolising the worldwide Anglican church today.

Continue the discussion with the children about the people and places their church has links with. Ask them to think about how they could simply illustrate this.

You will need

copies of the compasrose template

card

thread

pictures of places where the church has links

drawing materials

scissors

Blu-Tack

To make the mobile

* Cut out an enlargement of the compasrose illustration on card. Omit the mitre.

* At the eight points indicated secure eight pieces of thread so that they hang down from the compass.

* Ask the children to think of eight different places where they have links. They can draw a simple map of the country or place, design a symbol to illustrate it, or create a simple picture. These can then be hung from the mobile. If possible try to get some links outside this country. Try and make the eight pictures a similar size.

* The mobile can then be pinned to a ceiling or attached with Blu-Tack.

Patron Saints

An All-Age Presentation

Home-made patronal Tee-shirts. Photo: Dave Clark

Patronal festivals provide an opportunity for the church to remember the saint of their dedication and the 'saints' and holy men and women who have built up their church through its history. The patronal festival also provides a congregation with the reminder that they too are part of a continuing history, with a special role to play.

ACTIVITY IDEAS

Themes

These activities can form part of a special family service. They are all-age activities which aim to help people appreciate the history of their church and their part in that history.

The presentation, which is an 'ecclesiastical house that Jack built', is designed so that all can take part with little preparation. The material needs to be adapted to re-tell each church's own history.

Some churches might decide to augment the material. Local historians and schools could research the church's history and put on a display. The presentation could include costumes, music and lighting.

The Tee-shirts provide an opportunity for the children to learn more about their patron saint. By creating their own design children can find out about how their saint has been portrayed in Christian art.

Resources

Some well-known symbols of saints are illustrated here. A useful resource book for finding out more about Christian symbols is *Saints, Signs and Symbols - a Concise Dictionary* by W. Ellwood Post (SPCK).

Timing

The presentation needs advance planning. The teacher either needs to collect the items listed in the presentation or make posters with the children to illustrate each part of the presentation.

The Tee-shirt activity should be done a week in advance of the patronal festival and takes one or two sessions. The Tee-shirts could be worn during a patronal festival service.

1. A Patronal Presentation

You will need to choose a narrator to lead the congregation in telling the church's story and 10 people or more to hold up the illustrations. As each part of the text is narrated a person should come to the front of the church and hold up the item or poster listed.

1. This is the church where we go

2. This is the lady who cares for the church   Brush
   Where we go

3. This is the person who visits the village/town   Camera
   Who thanks the lady who cares for the church
   Where we go

4. This is the man who built the nave   Trowel
   Admired by the person who visits the village
   Who thanks the lady who cares for the church
   Where we go

5. This is the Bishop who died for his faith
   Who converted the man who built the nave
   Admired by the person who visits the village
   Who thanks the lady who cares for the church
   Where we go

Mitre

6. This is the man who translated the Bible
   Which inspired the Bishop who died for his faith
   Who converted the man who built the nave
   Admired by the person who visits the village
   Who thanks the lady who cares for the church
   Where we go

Bible

7. This is the King who defended the Cross
   Who encouraged the man who translated the Bible
   Which inspired the Bishop who died for his faith
   Who converted the man who built the nave
   Admired by the person who visits the village
   Who thanks the lady who cares for the church
   Where we go

Crown

8. This is the preacher who spoke about God
   Who baptised the King who defended the Cross
   Who encouraged the man who translated the Bible
   Which inspired the Bishop to die for his faith
   Who converted the man who built the nave
   Admired by the person who visits the village
   Who thanks the lady who cares for the church
   Where we go

Saint picture

9. And this is the Apostle who founded the church
   Which sent the preacher who spoke about God
   Who baptised the King who defended the cross
   Who encouraged the man who translated the Bible
   Which inspired the Bishop who died for his faith
   Who converted the man who built the nave
   Admired by the person who visits the village
   Who thanks the lady who cares for the church
   Where we go

Keys or
foundation
stone for
Peter

10. This is the one who offers New Life
    Who called the Apostle to found His Church
    Who touches the lips of the preacher who speaks
    Who through His spirit baptises the King
    Of whose words and deeds the Bible tells
    Who stood by the Bishop in the hour of death
    Who guided the craftsman builder's hands
    Who touched the visitor's heart with joy
    Who sees and is glad for the lady's care
    Who is with us now.

Cross

2. Patronal Tee-Shirts

Discussion

Find out with the children what the emblem is of the church's patron saint. If this is difficult tell the story of the saint to the children and let them think of a suitable symbol or emblem. They might decide to use one of the symbols illustrated here.

These instructions relate to fabric painting pens from the Early Learning Centre. If other paints are used follow the instructions on the product.

1. Ask the children to draw on a piece of paper a design for their patron saint Tee-shirt. They should use felt pens which are the same colour as the fabric pens. This ensures that the children have a clear idea about what they will do on the Tee-shirt before they use the fabric pens.

2. Make sure the Tee-shirts are washed and ironed first.

3. Put a protective piece of cardboard inside the Tee-shirt to stop the colour seeping through the whole Tee-shirt or onto the work surface. Secure this with pins so that the children have a secure surface to work on.

4. Use the fabric pens to paint a design straight onto the Tee-shirt. (teachers will need to help younger children with their design. Younger children can dap the pens to create spots on a previously drawn outline).

5. When the Tee-shirt is dry, remove the cardboard and cover the design with a clean (dispensable) cotton cloth.

6. Fix the colour by ironing each painted area for 1-2 minutes on the hottest setting suitable for that fabric.

You will need

old Tee-shirts or new plain Tee-Shirts

fabric painting pens or fabric paint with brushes

paper and felt pens

cardboard

pins

iron and board

overalls

newspaper to cover table

THE NATIONAL SOCIETY
A Christian Voice in Education

The National Society (Church of England) for Promoting Religious Education is a charity which supports all those involved in Christian education - teachers and school governors, students and parents, clergy and lay people - with the resources of its RE Centres, archives, courses and conferences.

Founded in 1811, the Society was chiefly responsible for setting up the nationwide network of Church schools in England and Wales and still provides grants for building projects and legal and administrative advice for headteachers and governors. It now publishes a wide range of books, pamphlets and audio-visual items, and two magazines *Crosscurrent* and *Together*.

For details of membership of the Society or to receive a copy of our current catalogue please contact the Promotions Secretary, The National Society, Church House, Great Smith Street, London SW1P 3NZ.

Related titles published by
National Society/Church House Publishing

Pick and Mix: Learning and Worship Ideas for All Ages

Edited by Margaret Dean

A major new anthology of active learning material with themes ranging from Ascension to Zeal. Over 250 activity suggestions to keep the most energetic church leader busy for years to come.

Step This Way: A Course for 5-7s in the Church

Edited by Marjorie Freeman

A whole year's course to use with the 5-7s in your church. Includes vivid stories especially written for this age group and attractive photocopyable TAKE IT HOME sheets.

Be a Church Detective: A Young Person's Guide to Old Churches

Clive Fewins. Cartoons by Taffy Davies

An introduction to the mysterious secrets of crypts, vaults, graveyards and towers for 8-14 year olds. Packed full of historical information, fact boxes, drawings and cartoons to encourage the junior "church crawler".

The Cher Khan
Stories

To Jude
Be lucky!

http://www.fast-print.net/bookshop

Chirp!!

Copyright © Suzahne Stewart 2016

Illustrations © Maggie Attfield

ISBN: 978-178456-341-7

First published 2015 by
FASTPRINT PUBLISHING
Peterborough, England.

CHIRP!!
An Introduction

These are the adventures of four animals and their friends...

Here is Cher Khan. He is a young ginger cat who is very vain and loves looking at himself.

This is Tabby. He is older and wiser, has a very kind heart, but is extremely GREEDY.

KoKo is a West Highland terrier who loves sorting out problems and...

...Blackbird is an excellent singer.

They all live in the village of Little Chirp.

In the nearby town of Chirp there is a circus, where other animals live and work. They are looked after extremely well and live in huge enclosures. We'll meet Raj and Taj, the tigers, who are brilliant dancers, but can sometimes be a bit scary!

Jamie and Leah are farmers. They make a good living from their farm and the wonderful food Leah cooks.

Dr Blister is the village vet. A good man who will always help any animal in need.

The animals all speak Animal Language. This is not difficult to learn, but most humans are too lazy to try. Young children can speak it, but most forget as they get older.

However, animals understand EVERYTHING that we say.

Enjoy their adventures and then colour in their pictures!

1

Trouble for Cher Khan

Cher Khan was in his garden eating a spider pie, when along came Tabby Cat, who poked him in the eye - and RAN OFF WITH HIS LUNCH!

"You rotten cat!" cried Cher Khan. Tabby had now run away ahead. Cher Khan set off after him and had nearly caught up with him when... "Ahhhh! I've fallen down a hole! Come back, Tabby. Help me. It's all your fault anyway. My leg! It's hurting so much." He started to cry from the pain.

Tabby stopped, dropping the spider pie He sat shame-faced for a moment. "I'm sorry," he said, moving foward. "It just looked so good and I'm always hungry."

"I'd have shared it with you if you'd asked," said Cher Khan angrily. "Now look at me!"

Tabby hung his head. "I'll call the other animals. See what they can do."

Soon afterwards KoKo and Blackbird arrived. KoKo looked scornfully at Tabby. "I knew your greed would cause problems one day." She inspected Cher Khan's leg. It had swollen to the size of a golf ball. "Well, we'll have to get you to Dr Blister," she said.

There was a silence.

"But how?" asked Tabby. "We have no money for a taxi."

Blackbird looked thoughtful and flew off. A few minutes later she returned.

"There is a skateboard belonging to a little boy across the road. His name is Laurie. We could borrow that."

The animals fetched the skateboard and helped Cher Khan on to it. They pushed it down the road with Blackbird flying ahead to warn of any potholes. They soon arrived at Dr Blister's Animal Hospital.

Dr Blister was a tall, fair-haired man with spectacles and twinkly blue eyes. It was well known that he would help any animal in trouble. His nurse, Esme, helped Cher Khan onto the examination couch.

"Right," he said. "I think it's just a sprain, but I'll have to make sure. I'm going to take a special photo – it's called an X-ray – and it will tell me if you have broken any bones."

"Can we be in the photo, too?" asked Blackbird eagerly.

"No," said the vet. "But you can watch through the window."

"Not much of a picture," said KoKo, staring in. "He didn't even ask Cher Khan to smile!"

3

Tabby wandered off.

"Good news," said the doctor, returning with a grey film. "It's just a strain. I'll bandage it up and you can go home. No jumping or tree-climbing for a few days."

Cher Khan returned to the skateboard and KoKo pushed it out.

"Where's Tabby?" asked Blackbird

"Must have gone home," replied Cher Khan.

In fact, Tabby had not gone home. He had noticed a plate of chocolates put out for the owners. "These look good," he said to himself, and ate the lot.

It was time for the surgery to close, but Tabby, feeling rather full, decided to have a little sleep. When he awoke it was almost dark and he was getting hungry again. He decided to look around for any tibits that had been left behind.

"My luck is in," he said to himself as he pawed open the fridge.

Inside was a whole cake. He tucked in happily, devouring most of it. "Time to go home, " he said, and jumped up to go through the window, He got halfway through... and stuck.

"Bother," he said, trying to wriggle through. But he couldn't, and he became completely wedged in. "What a stupid cat I am," he said, beginning to cry. Hours passed. It got very cold. At last, dawn broke and Nutcracker the squirrel wandered past.

"Help me, Nutcracker!" wailed Tabby. "I'm in a real mess."

"No way," replied the squirel. "I've heard all about you. Stealing food. You'll be after my nuts next!"

"I don't like nuts," lied Tabby, but Nutcracker had gone.

4

The next morning Dr Blister arrived at his surgery. He had a surprise for Esme, as it was her 21st birthday.

"Happy Birthday," he said. "There is a little treat for you in the fridge."

Esme was very excited until she looked into the fridge.

"There's nothing there," she said, mystified. "Apart from a plate of old crumbs."

"But there should be a birthday cake!" Dr Blister exclaimed, looking in. "Who has eaten it?"

"No need to ask," she replied. "Look who is in the window!"

Tabby squeaked.

"You naughty cat!" said Dr Blister. He was really angry. "You've completely ruined Esme's birthday surprise. I've a good mind to leave you where you are!"

Tabby whimpered. "I'm so sorry," he said. "It just looked so good."

"Yes," said the vet. "It was good, and now it's gone!"

"What can I do to make it up?" said Tabby. "I'll do anything."

Dr Blister pondered. "All right," he said. "I have some very important guests coming today. You will push plates of delicious chocolate biscuits around. If you ever so much as lick one, you will never be allowed in my surgery again."

"What a punishment," said Tabby. "Yes, and it's well deserved."

With that, Dr Blister picked up the phone to order another cake from Leah.

Summer Fayre

Every year in the village of Little Chirp there was a Summer Fayre and all the villagers and their animals attended. There was a tombola stall, homemade cakes, a raffle, bouncy castle and entertainments, usually in the form of a talent show and an animal beauty contest. Everyone hoped for good weather and this year they weren't disappointed.

"Let's sing them a song," suggested Cher Khan to the others. "We might win a prize."

"Good idea," said KoKo. "What about 'Hey Diddle Diddle?'"

Tabby nodded in agreement.

All three animals marched onto the stage whilst Blackbird perched on a fence, her head on one side, watching curiously. A crowd gathered to watch.

"Right," said Koko. "A one, two, three, four…"

They all started singing, apart from Blackbird. The noise was unbelievably awful. None of them could sing a single note in tune. "Grwwwwwwww,weeeeeeeee, miaoooooo." They whined on and on.

"What on earth are they singing?" asked a man in the crowd. "Sounds like Three Blind Mice after they've had their tails cut off."

"Rubbish!" said another.

"BOOOOOOOOOOOO! GET OFF THE STAGE!" the crowd shouted.

Someone threw a half-eaten sandwich at them. Tabby immediately wolfed it down. The others looked on scornfully. "No point in wasting good food," he said.

"They don't like us," said KoKo with tears in her eyes. "They think we're rubbish!"

"That's because you are," said Blackbird, hovering overhead. "Shut up, and let me take over!" She started to sing a very sweet chorus and the people, who had been moving away, stopped to listen. What they didn't know was that she was calling her friends, the Wren Family. Soon, half-a-dozen birds were singing in perfect harmony.

"Let's help," said KoKo. "I'll beat time on this little box. Cher Khan, you dance. Tabby, there's an empty baked bean tin over there. Push it around on our cart and see if we can make some money."

Tabby did just that, although he did pause to lick the tin clean. It soon began to fill with pennies, 10p's and even the odd 50p.

"We've all done brilliantly," said Cher Khan.

"Thanks to the birds," KoKo reminded him.

The Wren family took a swift bow and flew off.

Next was the Beauty Contest. The judging took place and the Lord Mayor stepped forward to announce the winners.

"Very high standard this year, from all entrants." he said. "But the prize for Best Kept Dog goes to.. .KoKo!"

Everybody clapped and the Mayor fixed a diamond-studded collar on KoKo's neck. She preened herself.

"Next, for the bird with the shiniest feathers. Without a doubt, it's Blackbird. She gets to wear a medal, The Order of The Beak of England." He placed it around her neck and she cooed happily.

"And lastly... Best and Prettiest Cat. Very difficult again, but... it goes to... Cher Khan." He took a beautifully crafted gold crown from a box and placed it on Cher Khan's head.

"Yippee!" cried Cher Khan, prancing around with delight. "Yippee! Yipee! I'm a King! I'm a King! I'm King of the Khans!"

Tabby looked on sullenly. He had won nothing.

"Never mind, Tabby," said Cher Khan. "Always next year. You're a bit tubby... maybe a bit of a diet might help? I'm King Khan! I'm King Khan..."

Tabby slunk away with his tail between his legs.

Cher Khan was so engrossed in his newfound fame and his crown that he did not notice two enormous shadows creeping up behind him.

"So...You're the King of the Khans, are you?" growled a loud deep voice. "I think not."

Two huge tigers had appeared from nowhere. "How DARE you say that you are king of the mighty Tribe of Khan?" One of the tigers flipped Cher Khan up with a single twist of his tail into the nearest tree. The other looked at him threateningly.

"I'm sorry! I'm sorry!" Cher Khan cried. "I didn't know."

Well, that was what he meant to say, but all that came out was a little chirp. He quivered in the tree.

The tiger growled again, but this time more softly.

"Let me introduce myself," he said, "I am Raj Khan, true King of the Khans, and this is my wife, Taj. We are highly skilled performing tigers in the circus and we don't take kindly to other animals pretending to be us."

"He's very young, Raj," said Taj. "Hardly more than a kitten. It's not his fault if some silly people call him King Khan. I remember what you used to be like at his age." She looked at him meaningfully.

"Hmmm," said Raj. "I suppose it's not your fault." He pondered. "Well, your ginger stripes are very clear and your coat is in excellent condition. I guess you could be some sort of king." He spoke to his wife, who nodded. "All right," he said at last. "You can be The Orange King, or King of The Oranges. But you are NOT one of us and never can be. You are just a ginger cat and a very silly one at that. If we hear that you telling people that you are a tiger king again, we won't be as forgiving. In fact, we will make mincemeat of you."

"Not mincemeat," said Taj. "Marmalade." They turned and strolled away.

Tabby had been sitting on a fence laughing till the tears ran down down his whiskers. Cher Khan stared. "Tabby...how did you know how to contact these beasts?" he demanded.

"Well," Tabby replied. "Let's just say it's nice to keep these things in the family!" He gave him a wink and waddled off in search of his dinner.

The Seaside

"**W**hat shall we do with our money?" said KoKo. "There's quite a bit." It was true. The people of Little Chirp had given generously.

"How about a really slap-up meal at Friendly Frank's Fresh Fried Fish and Fantasy Frizzles?" suggested Tabby, licking his lips.

"No!" said the other animals in unison.

"Well, not all our money," said Cher Khan. "Let's use half to have a special treat. How about a day at the seaside?"

"Good idea," said Blackbird.

They queued up for the local bus to Chirp-on-Sea.

"I've heard all about you animals," said the driver severely as they got on board. "Larking around. Making a noise. Earning good money, too, so I've been told. Well, as long as only Blackbird sings, I'll let you on board. But any funny business with you other animals and you're

off." He sounded gruff, but there was a twinkle in his eyes.

The sun was shining brightly on Chirp Beach as the animals got off the bus. Lots of people lay around on sunbeds sipping drinks and eating sandwiches. Some were building sand-castles with their children.

"Hey, it's Laurie!" said Tabby, pointing to the little boy whose skateboard they'd borrowed when they took Cher Khan to Dr Blister. "Hi, Laurie!"

The little boy waved in delight. "Hello, animals. I'm going paddling in a rock pool."

"Well, we're going on a pedalo," said Tabby. "Me and Cher Khan. Blackbird has gone to see her friends, the seagulls, and KoKo is going to have a little swim."

Laurie picked up his bucket and began to hunt for crabs.

"This is the life," said Tabby to Cher Khan as they drifted along in the sunshine. The sea was as flat as a millpond and they stretched out, admiring the views of Chirp Forest.

Suddenly, there was a rumble in the sky. KoKo, swimming along beside them, said anxiously, "There's going to be a storm, I think."

"No. You're imagining it," said Tabby. "It's really calm!"

He spoke too soon. All at once a huge wave swept in towards the beach. In the rockpool where Laurie was playing it lifted him up and started to sweep him out to sea. He began to scream, but the wind took his cries away.

"My goodness!" squeaked Blackbird. "He's going to drown! WE MUST HELP! AT ONCE!"

"How?" shouted Cher Khan. "We can't swim."

"Well, do SOMETHING!"

Both cats stood up in the pedalo, which wobbled dangerously in the sea. They swished their tails as hard as they could to try and attract attention.

"I'm coming, Laurie!" shouted KoKo to the terrified toddler, who was being dragged further and further out to sea. It was no use.

"I can't make it. I can only do the dog paddle," she panted.

Blackbird swooped down. She had seen what was happening and tried to speak to Laurie's parents, Mr and Mrs Driver, but they were busy doing crosswords.

"Oh dear," said Blackbird to herself. "If only more humans would learn Animal Language. It's not hard. They call us dumb animals, but it's they who are dumb! We understand everything they say. I really don't want to do this, but..." She flew to a great height to dive down, pecking Mr Driver as hard as she could on his cheek. Blood spurted out of the gash.

"What the...that wretched bird!" he said to his wife. "Look what it's done!" He patted a tissue to his face. Blackbird, meanwhile, was making a furious attempt to grab the Drivers' attention by flapping her wings. Mrs Driver suddenly took notice of her efforts. "Where's Laurie?" she said. "He was in the pool. Oh, my goodness! HELP! HELP!" she screamed, seeing her little boy being washed away.

Mr Driver rushed into the sea. The coldness of the water made him gasp, but he struck out, passing KoKo, who sighed in relief. In no time he reached Laurie, who had twice been pulled under the water. The little boy coughed and spluttered. His cheeks were bright red and his skin was covered in goosebumps. As gently as he could, Mr Driver carried him back to the shore, tears streaming down his face.

"Another few moments, Laurie would have drowned," he said to his wife, who had also started to cry. "That bird! Those animals! They KNEW something was up. That bird pecked me to get our attention."

Blackbird, Cher Khan, Tabby and KoKo, all safely back onshore, were sitting huddled together, the enormity of what might have happened beginning to sink in. They shivered with shock, but were happy that the boy had been saved.

"That blackbird is amazing," said Mrs Driver. "We've seen you in our garden before," she said to Blackbird. "From now on, for the rest of your life, you will always have a rasher of bacon every day. We can never thank you enough. As for you other animals – we'll find a way to reward you, too."

Tabby pricked up his ears and licked his lips expectantly.

"Don't say it," said Cher Khan "You were going to ask for a rasher of bacon, too, weren't you?"

"Well...I suppose...Oh well, we still have half our money left over for a trip to Friendly Frank's. I really fancy some Fantasy Frizzles."

"What are they?" asked Cher Khan.

"Well, Frank makes this fantastic batter and you can have anything tasty fried in it. My favourite is Worms and Worcester Sauce."

"Worms all around then," said KoKo. "And I quite fancy a spider pie, too."

A Good Night's Work

Jamie and Leah lived in Little Chirp Farm in the village. They owned KoKo, as well as the fifty chickens they kept to provide eggs for the village shop.

Leah was a wonderful cook, and she and Jamie grew most of their vegetables. There were tomatoes, beans, radishes and potatoes, as well as fruit such as strawberries, plums, pears, apples and cherries.

Jamie and Leah made a living from the farm, as well as from Leah's cooking for dinner parties using all the best and freshest ingredients. She made delicious soups, stews, pies, salads, jams, chutneys and, of course, egg dishes.

Then one day a terrible thing happened. When Leah got up one morning to collect the eggs for the village shop she saw feathers strewn all over the path to the coops, and then, as she followed the path, she saw that some of the chickens had been killed. In fact, quite a lot of them. She gave a scream of horror that brought Jamie running to see what the matter was.

"Our chickens!" howled Leah. "Someone has killed them. Everyone loved the taste of their eggs, especially the rare birds' ones. We loved them, and they bought us in money. What are we going to do?"

Jamie was stunned. "How could anyone do this to us and our animals? What shall we do?"

KoKo had been watching. She hated to see Leah in tears and Jamie so upset. She jumped into Leah's lap and put her paw on her face to dry her tears. If only she could speak Animal Language, she thought.

KoKo had an idea and went off to see Tabby. She thought that the raid had been caused by foxes, who loved to kill chickens.

Now, as we know, Tabby had a special link with the tigers. He listened hard as KoKo told him what had happened. "Right," he said, "let's see what we can do to help."

KoKo was right. That night there were two foxes out for another night of fun. They hung around the house until they saw the Jamie and Leah had gone to bed.

"Now, let's get the rest," said the first fox. "Come on. There's some sport here tonight!"

But he spoke too soon. As he reached the first chicken coop there was a low growl. "What was that?" he said to his friend. "Don't know," the other fox replied. "Come on."

15

"Grrrrrrw. Oh no you don't! You rotten animals! You didn't even need the chickens for food," said one of the tigers, who had appeared from nowhere. "You did it all just for fun. You had no need to hunt. You are despicable, taking the livelihood from these people. You need to be punished. And you are going to be."

Raj and Taj each picked up a fox by the scruff of its neck, and none too gently at that either. "You are coming with us, and you are not going to like it," said Taj.

The animals returned to the circus, where Raj put them into empty cages, then pushed the bolts through. The foxes were crying by now, but the tigers took no notice. "A good night's work," said Raj.

Next morning, the keeper came around as usual with the animals' breakfasts. At once he saw the foxes and couldn't believe his eyes.

"Wow!" he said. "I've never known animals get INTO cages before. It must be because you want to join the circus."

He thought for a while. "But you have no skills. We don't even know if we can train you. Hmm, I suppose we could give you a trial, just to see if you are up to circus life. You can begin by mucking out the animals' enclosures. Let's start with the tigers. There is always a lot of poo there!"

Hello, RK

"**I** am rather worried about my wife," said Raj to the keeper. "She's been sick a few times, off her food and rather grumpy. Very unlike her usual chirpy self. She also seems to have tummy pains now and then." The keeper listened and went to see the tigress. It was true. She lay languidly on one side, a plate of bangers and mash untouched, and her favourite bacon and strawberry smoothie hadn't even been sniffed.

"Right," said the keeper. "Time to give Dr Blister a call. This might be serious!"

Twenty minutes later, the vet arrived with his medicine bag.

"Poor old girl," he said to Taj. "May I examine you? I'll do my best not to hurt."

The tigress groaned in pain and sweat started to pour down her face as Dr Blister felt her tummy. He looked thoughtful. "You've never had anything like this before?" he asked. Taj shook her head. "Well, I know what it is, and the pain is going to stop very soon, but I just need to speak to your husband and the keeper first." He walked out to meet their anxious faces.

"OK, Taj will not be able to dance on stage for a few days." The keeper looked dismayed. "But the good news is... that she is about to give birth to a cub!"

"What?" said Raj and the keeper together, stunned. "A cub?" repeated Raj. "How can this possibly have happened?"

"Oh, I think nature must have taken its course one evening," said the vet, with a twinkle in his eyes. "Now, there is no time to lose. I need some very hot water and some soft fluffy towels as soon as possible."

"But what can I do?" said Raj. "Hold her paw or something? I'm new to this!"

"You just pace up and down outside the sleeping shelter," said the vet. "That's what a lot of new fathers do. Leave the rest to me."

Hours seemed to pass as Raj waited anxiously. "Why is everything taking so long? Why won't Dr Blister let me see her? I hope she's not in too much pain," he muttered. After what seemed like ages, Dr Blister came from the sleeping shelter with a small bundle, wrapped in one of the towels. He looked exhausted.

"You have a beautiful son," he said. "He took his time coming into the world, and your wife is very tired. She has fed him, and can't wait to see you, then she needs a good sleep. Come on."

Raj peeked at the bundle as Dr Blister carried it back to Taj. He curled up beside her and the vet took away the towel. Raj bent forward and... gasped in horror.

"It's BLIND!" he said. "My son is BLIND!"

Dr Blister laughed. "No, no, no," he said. "All cats, large or small, are born with their eyes closed for the first week or two. Lets them get used to the world."

The relief on Raj's face was unbelievable. He bent forward to kiss his wife, who was now purring gently. "You've given me a beautiful son, my princess. What shall we call him?"

Taj pondered. She wanted to go to sleep. "I think, Rajeev, after you. Bengal, after my father, and then Khan, the family name. What do you think?"

"Hello, Rajeev," said Raj, touching the cub's cheek with his huge paw. "Taj, you have made me so happy today." He turned away as tears of joy had sprung into his eyes. "I can't wait for us to have another child. Maybe a daughter next time?"

Taj gave a little shudder. "Give me a chance, Raj," she said. "We've only just had him."

"Let her rest now," said Dr Blister. "Word will soon get out that there has been a new addition to the circus, and no doubt the newspapers and TV crew will be in touch."

18

He was right. Mercury, the racing pigeon, told all the village animals and the keeper alerted the Daily Chirp and Chirp TV the next day. Crowds began to gather for the pictures, as this was the first time a cub had been born in the circus.

"What a lot of cameras!" said Cher Khan to Tabby. "Do you think that we may be able to be in a picture, too?"

"Well, let us all push our way to the front!" replied Tabby, "otherwise, we definitely won't be!" The four animals edged in. A cameraman took photos of them with the cub and his parents. He then transferred them onto a computer screen and showed them around.

"Much better than Dr Blister's photos," said Koko. "His are always grey and only show shadows and bones!"

The people in the crowd all cheered and clapped as the tiger family left for their lunch, but there were two people among them who were clapping for very different reasons.

Playground

Cher Khan was bored. KoKo had gone on holiday with her owners, Jamie and Leah. Blackbird had gone to visit relatives in the nearby village of Little Peck and Tabby had just finished a huge lunch of eggs, bacon, sausages and fried bread. He lay on a sun lounger snoring loudly.

"It's a lovely day and there is no one to play with," he grumbled to himself. "I wonder if anything is going on at the playground." He trotted off to see.

"It can't be. It's Rajeev Khan, the tiger cub, playing on the swings. Where are his parents? Surely he is far too young to be let out on his own? He's only a few months old. What can the keeper be thinking of? Do his mother and father know?"

"Hello, Cher Khan," said Rajeev, waving. "Will you push me? I want to go higher and higher!"

"Do your mum and dad know you're here? Surely you should be back at the tiger enclosure?"

"Oh no," said Rajeev. "They're practising a new dance routine and I slipped out whilst no one was looking." He chuckled mischievously. "It was a piece of cake."

Cher Khan felt nervous. "We must get you back to the enclosure," he said. "You really shouldn't be here."

"Just one more swing ride," Rajeev said. "Come on, Cher Khan. Give me a push."

Suddenly Cher Khan sensed danger. His hackles rose and he looked around fearfully. Nothing.

Then he glimpsed the glint of a binocular lens. Cher Khan froze.

"Get away, Rajeev! Get away! Someone is after you!"

"What?" The cub stared at him.

"NOW! HUNTERS!" He pushed Rajeev off the swing. A shot rang out and Rajeev, screaming in terror, ran away, Cher Khan close behind.

Cher Khan was not so lucky. A second shot rang out and caught him in his side as he tried to shield the cub. "I've been shot!" he yelled in agony. "HELP! HELP! Get Dr Blister. Get Dr Blizz..." He managed a few more paces and fell unconscious to the ground. His gold crown fell off and rolled into the bushes.

"YOU FOOL!" said the first hunter. "You've missed the tiger cub. All you did was shoot an ordinary ginger cat. I should never have trusted you with that gun!"

"But he was wearing a gold crown," said the other man. "It must be worth quite a lot of money, especially as the price of gold is so high. Let's find it."

"All right," the other hunter said, worried, "but let's get a move on. Someone may have seen something."

Meanwhile, Rajeev had managed to get back to the tiger enclosure. "Where on earth have you been?" exclaimed his mother, Taj, loudly. "We were worried sick. Anything could have happened to you!"

Tears started to flow down the cub's face and whiskers. "Actually, it did," he said and described what had happened at the playground.

"WHAT...!" Raj's growl was so loud that even Taj took a step back. "YOU STUPID BOY! Don't you realise how rare and valuable we are? Now, because of your idiotic behaviour you have risked the life of an innocent animal. Maybe you are even responsible for his death. What are we going to do?" He looked at his wife. "We can't leave him. He's one of us. Well, almost one of us."

"We can't do anything ourselves, Raj," said Taj, thinking. "We're performing tonight. But what about one of the pigeons?"

"Pigeons!" he snapped back. "They are performing, too."

"Yes, but not until the second half. We could get a message to Dr Blister. Mercury would be the best bird. He used to be a racing pigeon."

Dr Blister was preparing treatment plans for the next day's patients when he heard a firm tapping on the window. "Oh, hi, Mercury," he said. "What brings you here?"

"Bad news, I'm afraid," replied the bird.

Dr Blister listened in horrified silence as Mercury explained. "I have to fly," said Mercury when he'd delivered his message. "I'm on stage later. The show must go on!"

"Esme," Dr Blister said to his nurse. "Call the police. Tell them that one of the village animals has been shot, maybe even killed, and that the tiger cub was nearly kidnapped. I'm going down to the playground now in the Animal Ambulance." He snatched up his medical bag.

As soon as he arrived at the playground he saw the still body of Cher Khan lying with his eyes half open. "Oh no!" he said. "I'm too late." Tears glistened in his eyes, and he took out a towel to cover him up. As he did so, there was a small twitch in Cher Khan's tail.

"My goodness! Perhaps he isn't dead!" Quickly, Dr Blister felt for a pulse and checked his breathing.

YES..." Very, very gently he picked Cher Khan up and put him in the ambulance. He fixed an oxygen mask on him to help him breathe. "I think I know what has happened," he said to himself. He filled a syringe and injected the cat in his leg. Then he sat back to wait.

The police had arrived at the scene and were looking for the hunters. They saw two men sauntering around, enjoying the sunshine.

"We have had reports of an assault and a kidnap," said the officer. "Seen anything?"

"No. Not at all. Did you see anything, Fred?"

"Not a bean," replied his friend. "Not a bean."

"Why are you standing so closely in front of those bushes?" asked the policeman.

The men looked shifty.

"Officer, I ..."

"Search him. And look in those bushes," the officer told his colleague. They soon found two rifles and Cher Khan's gold crown.

"Right,"said the first policeman. "This crown was worn by a local cat that has been reported injured. And an atttempt was made to kidnap the tiger cub." He took out his notebook.

"We are arresting you for:

Attempted kidnap

Attempted murder

Unlawful possession of firearms and,

Theft of a gold crown. "

"Don't forget parking on double yellow lines, too," said the other policeman.

"Of course. Very serious that. Well, you will be going to prison for a very long time," he said, getting out the handcuffs. "Into the car. And don't try to struggle, or it will be the worse for you!"

"Where am I?" asked Cher Khan groggily. "What's happened?"

"You were very lucky," said Dr Blister. "The hunters wanted the tiger cub and fired at him with a dart which would make him go into a deep sleep – an anaesthetic. It was far too strong for you and nearly killed you. You are all right now, but we are going to keep you in the hospital tonight in case you feel ill." Cher Khan dropped back to sleep.

The next day, he was awoken by the tap-tap-tapping of Mercury's beak on the window.

"I have a message for you from the tigers," he said. "It is: Please come to our enclosure soon. We can't come out at the moment."

Cher Khan sauntered into the enclosure later on that morning. He felt a lot better. Raj and Taj were waiting for him.

"We can never thank you enough for saving Rajeev from goodness knows what fate,

maybe even death. We can never make it up to you, but...we would like to give you a title." Raj touched Cher Khan's shoulders lightly with his enormous paw.

"From now on, you will be Cher Khan, Honorary Warrior Tiger (Highest Order).

Cher Khan blushed with so much pride that his coat turned as red as it could get. "Thank you," was all he managed to say.

"Now, would you care to join us for lunch? Today we're having Cornish pasties."

Berry-Picking

Jamie was enjoying his breakfast egg and glancing at the local paper. Something caught his eye and he read it out to Leah, who was busily preparing menus for her next dinner party.

> Reports have come in that a wild beast has been spotted in Chirp Forest. It
> is said that it is about the size of a large cow and should not be approached
> under any circumstances as it is thought to be dangerous.

"Hhmm," said Jamie. "Well, we go there often and we've never seen anything." KoKo listened intently.

"Hello, it's Khan here. Anyone coming out to play?" There was no response. Ever since he had been made an Honorary Warrior Tiger (Highest Order), he had taken to calling himself 'Khan.'

The others ignored him when he did this.

"It's The Orange King. Anyone around?"

Silence.

"Bother," said Cher Khan. "Why can't anyone use my titles?"

On the other side of the fence Tabby grumbled, "He'll be wanting us to call him Mr Khan next."

"It's Cher Khan. Who wants to play?"

At once three heads popped up over the fence.

"Hello, CHER Khan. We were just talking about going into Chirp Forest and looking for berries. Fancy coming along?"

"Great! I'll get the basket on wheels so that we won't have to carry them," he said.

All four animals proceeded to the forest and started to pick wild berries. The sun was shining and they worked happily together, throwing all sorts of soft fruit into the basket.

"What's that funny yellowish blob in the bushes?" said Blackbird. "I thought it moved." She flew overhead to see what she could find.

The other animals inched in. They, too, had seen something, but they didn't know what it was.

It struck KoKo that it might be The Beast, but she dismissed this thought as it wasn't the size of a large cow.

As they got nearer they were startled by a loud hiss. Cher Khan thought that it could have been a snake, but then A Thing emerged from the bushes, and it certainly wasn't a snake.

An enormous blob of stinking yellowish hair was heading for them. It had bloodshot amber eyes and weeping scabs all over its matted body. It limped as it scratched at its sores. From its mouth dribbled a foul smelling fluid and its nose was encrusted with an unclean mess.

"How dare you come to my part of the forest!" it hissed. "What do you want? If you try to hurt me you will be very sorry indeed. I am extremely strong. And look at all my sharp teeth!" It opened its mouth to reveal yellow rotting fangs.

The animals stood rooted to the spot, very afraid. Every hair on their backs tingled. Finally, Tabby brushed up his courage and spoke.

"We mean you no harm, Beast. We are all animals, too. Why are you here? What are you? We promise not to harm you."

There was a long silence. The Beast moved back a pace or two. It looked very ill. Finally, it spoke. "I am a Long-Haired Cat," it said eventually.

Cher Khan and Tabby looked at each other. It certainly didn't look like a cat.

"Yes," the creature repeated. "I am a girl cat. I used to have owners, but they abandoned me. Twice. They took me down to the playground, but I managed to find my way home. Then, I had a pain in my tummy and was sick on the floor, and the children started hitting me with a stick and threw stones at me. The puppy bit me, too. Then my owners left me in the woods. I've been here for ages. Everyone hates me and there is not much food. There are also lots of nasty insects around that bite. My name is Custard Fleabag. It used to just be Custard, because of my yellowish fur, but after they left me in the playground, I got fleas as well." The cat whimpered a little.

The animals looked at each other in horror and they all took a step forward.

"Don't you try and hurt me, too," she said. "I really am very strong."

She bent forward and tried to stand, but was so weak that she fell over. The animals stared at her.

"There's only one thing to be done," said Cher Khan at last.

"Yes. We have no choice," said KoKo.

"She's going to die," said Tabby.

"DON'T YOU COME NEAR ME!" screamed Custard Fleabag. "I am a really fierce fighter!"

"We want to help you," said Blackbird, who had re-appeared. "We are going to take you to our friend, Dr Blister, an animal doctor, and he will make you well again. We promise no harm will come to you. Now, Cher Khan, chuck out those berries and help Custard Fleabag into the basket. She's too weak to walk."

Not long after, they arrived at Dr Blister's surgery. He listened to them and looked grave as he took in Custard Fleabag's condition.

"Right," he said. "The first thing is that my nurse Esme will give you a warm bath. Then we'll deal with your coat and the little infections that you have picked up."

Custard Fleabag didn't really like the bath, but felt better after. Then Dr Blister took two hours cutting out her matted fur balls and combing out as much hair as he could without hurting her.

"Now," he said "I'm going to put a little ointment around your neck. That will get rid of the fleas. Then, some drops in your ears and eyes to stop the infections. After that, I will dress the sores and scabs that you have and you will immediately feel a whole lot better. You are in luck tonight. I have a huge pot of excellent stew that Leah from the farm made for me and the family, and I'm sure we can find enough for you. Then, I will try to find you a new home."

Custard Fleabag was in tears. "No one has ever been this kind to me before. I can't believe this is happening." She tucked into the stew whilst Dr Blister went off to make some phone calls.

"Good news and bad news, I'm afraid," said Dr Blister as he returned a few minutes later.

"I'm sorry, but I can't find you any new owners." The cat hung her head "I knew things were too good to be true," she said.

"However," continued Dr Blister, "how would you like a job?"

"A job!" exclaimed the cat. "Who would want to give me a job? And what would I do?"

"I'm offering you a job," said Dr Blister. " Would you like to be caretaker to my surgery? You would just need to keep a watch on doors and windows, and maybe have a little chat with any animals that are staying overnight in the hospital. If there is an emergency, there is a red button that will connect you to me. In return, you will get a comfy place to sleep, friends, good food, and if you are ill I will make you better. What do you say?"

Custard Fleabag looked overwhelmed.

"Yes, yes and yes. Thank you so much."

"And another thing," said Dr Blister. "Your coat will grow back and you will again be the beautiful animal that you once were. Custard Fleabag is not a nice name at all, and you have stunning amber eyes. We are going to rename you CARAMEL EYES."

And with that, he went off to enjoy his own plate of stew.

Christmas Eve

It was Christmas Eve in the village of Little Chirp. It had been snowing heavily, but whilst the main roads had been gritted, most of the village was thick with snow. Cher Khan, Tabby and KoKo were watching Mrs Driver wrap up a final few Christmas presents. Mrs Driver had kept her promise to Blackbird about always making a good meal available to her everyday, and Blackbird was now snug in her nest after feeding her family with bacon rashers and other tasty leftover treats.

"Wow!" said Tabby. "Look at that cake!" He licked his lips greedily. The tree looked beautiful with shimmering lights, baubles and a fairy on the top. The fairy saw the animals in the window and winked at them before waving her wand – and dropping it. Scowling, she tried to retrieve it, but she slipped and fell off the top of the tree.

"Stupid fairy!" said Cher Khan. "I could do much better. She can't even climb back up!" He adjusted his gold crown.

"Look at the presents!" exclaimed KoKo. "There a lovely watch, chocolates and someone is going to get an X-Box."

"What is an X-Box?" asked Cher Khan. The others looked at him.

"Well... it's a, it's a, well, it can't be much good, otherwise everyone would have one," said Tabby knowingly.

Mrs Driver finished wrapping a few more little gifts for under the tree. "Right," she said to herself, "time to pick up Laurie from playschool." She fetched her coat and went off to her car, but as she drove off she didn't notice a van coming from the opposite direction. It stopped outside her front door.

Two nasty-looking men got out hurriedly with sacks. One had a hammer and a crowbar. "OK," said the first one, "let's clean this place out of Christmas presents before she comes back. Look sharp. We don't have much time." The other robber nodded. The hammer and crowbar were raised to force a window.

The animals looked at each other in horror. What were they to do? "We must get hold of the police at once," said Cher Khan. "KoKo, get down there, quickly."

"But they can't speak Animal Language," replied the dog.

"One does. Sergeant Bark. He's the Police Dog Trainer. Quickly now, and I'll try to divert them. Tabby ...you can... Tabby? Where are you?"

Tabby was nowhere to be seen. "Drat," said Cher Khan. "That wretched animal is never

31

around when we need him." KoKo shot off.

Just then, a snowball landed squarely in the face of the first robber.

"Why did you do that?" he asked his partner in crime.

"I didn't," the other robber said.

Whoosh. Another snowball hit the second robber.

"Why are you doing this?" he asked.

Neither of them had seen that Cher Khan had raced up a tree and was throwing snowballs as hard and as fast as he could. The robbers started to argue.

"This place must be haunted. There has to be a ghost." Robber No 1 took a brick from his bag, but as he was about to throw it into the window there was a loud thud. A snowball had hit him squarely on the nose.

"What on earth did you do that for?" he asked.

"Do what?" said the other robber.

"Arrrggh! Why are you chucking snowballs at me?"

"I'm not."

"Crikey! Who is it then? There's no one around. It must be you."

"No, it isn't."

Another snowball hit him hard on his ample tummy. "It is you."

They were so engrossed in their argument that they didn't see two huge shadows creeping into the garden.

"Can't be a ghost," said his friend. "The graveyard is miles away, and has had a factory built on it anyway.

"I'm SCARED," said the first one. Another snowball hit him in the face. "Let's get out of here fast!"

But before they could move the robbers found themselves staring into the huge yellow eyes of the tigers, Raj and Taj. They screamed, but it was too late. Effortlessly, each tiger pinned a robber down with a huge paw. Snarling, they struck them to the ground and sat on them, with their claws extended. Tabby stood in the background, grinning. Suddenly, there was the sound of a police siren and two cars pulled up.

"Ohh, we are so glad to see you! Help us! We need your help. Badly." The policemen looked baffled. "We have come to arrest you for attempted burglary, and you say you want our help? Are you mad?"

"Tttttttt… ttttt… tigers. Tigers were trying to kill us. You must believe us. Tigers."

The officers smirked. "Oh yeah? Tigers? You must think we're stupid. Tigers, indeed. Tigers mainly live in hot countries, not in snow. And you are in big trouble," one of the officers said, glancing at his companion. "Tigers!" he mocked. "They'll be saying that animals can talk next!" Sergeant Bark allowed himself a secret grin as the robbers were taken away. It had started to snow heavily again. The tigers were nowhere to be seen.

Love, Santa

It was very late on the night of Christmas Eve. Caramel Eyes had checked all the windows and doors in the surgery and sat back to preen her luxurious, perfectly groomed winter coat. There were no animals in the hospital that night, and as she washed her paws she looked forward to a nice long lie-in the next morning. Suddenly, there was a scuffling noise around the surgery chimney.

"Drat!" said Caramel Eyes to herself. "It must be that rotten rat family turning up again. And I thought that I'd dealt with them once and for all after their antics last time!"

The scuffle continued, and Caramel Eyes braced herself to deal with the intruders. She fluffed up her fur, drew her claws and prepared to pounce. Silence. Then a grubby torn red bobble hat fell down the chimney. Her eyes grew as round as saucers.

"Oh, bother, bother and bother!" said a voice. A dirty figure emerged from the grate. The red suit was torn, the grey beard was streaked with soot, the man had a cut on his face and one of his round-eyed spectacles had cracked. Caramel Eyes was surprised that he spoke Animal Language.

"And who might you be?" said Caramel Eyes. "Creeping around at this time of night! I suppose you'd like me to think that you're Santa Claus!"

The man pondered. "Actually, I am," he said. "I have had a bit of a mishap with the sledge and, as I was flying past, I saw the sign for Dr Blister's Animal Surgery." He wiped a grimy hand over his forehead.

"Oh yeah?" said Caramel Eyes. "And do you really think I believe you? Santa Claus is a nice old chap with a sack full of presents and a sledge pulled by reindeer. You look like an old tramp!"

"I agree," said Santa, "but my sledge has been hit by a shooting star and I need to deliver the presents. One of my reindeers has been hurt. I HAVE to see Dr Blister."

Caramel Eyes was silent for a moment. "Maybe I believe you. Maybe I don't. But if you mean Dr Blister or any of his family any harm, then you will have me to answer to. And make no mistake, you don't want me as an enemy."

"Oh, do hurry," said Santa. "I really do have a very busy night ahead."

"All right," said Caramel Eyes. "But remember...!" Reluctantly, she pushed the red emergency button to call Dr Blister.

A few minutes later he walked into the surgery in his pyjamas and rubbing his eyes. "What the ...?"

"Yes," said Santa. "It's me. We have a problem. Prancer, one of my reindeer, has been injured. Can you help?"

Astonished, Dr Blister listened as Santa related what had happened. "OK," he said. "Let's see what we can do."

Dr Blister and Santa walked outside to the sledge and helped Prancer into the surgery. She whimpered with pain as Dr Blister examined her. "Right," he said, "I need to stitch up a long gash on her leg and take some photos – X-rays – to see that nothing has been broken. I'm afraid she will not be flying for a good few weeks."

"What?" said Santa, aghast. "But it's Christmas Eve. I can't let all the children down."

"Sorry," said Dr Blister firmly. "This animal is not leaving my surgery tonight. If she flies, then she will never 'prance' again."

"But what will I do!" wailed Santa, wringing his hands.

"Well, they have tigers at the circus," said Caramel Eyes.

"Great!" said Santa, snorting. "They'll probably see my reindeer as their breakfast!" .

35

"Or there is an elephant. Her name is Nellie."

"An elephant?" he said. "Are you having a laugh? An elephant would never get the sledge off the road."

"Let me make a phone call," said Dr Blister. He picked up the phone.

"Jamie? Is that you?" Jamie didn't sound at all pleased to be woken up. His voice was heavy with sleep.

"Dr Blister? Why are you calling so late? We have both been working extremely hard in the run-up to Christmas."

"I know. I'm sorry. But we have a huge problem. It's Santa and his sledge!"

"What!" exclaimed Jamie. "Santa has broken down? Doesn't he have breakdown cover? The RAC or the AA? I know that I can fix a lot of things, but I've never done a sledge. Is it the bells? I could probably mend those."

"No," said Dr Blister, trying to remain patient. "Did you manage to get that little present for Leah that we talked about?"

"Well yes, but she is very small. What is this all about anyway?"

"Jamie, we need you and her. If you can't help no one will get any presents tonight." He explained the problem and half an hour later Jamie turned up with a horse box containing a very small reindeer. Dr Blister examined her carefully.

"Well, she IS very small, but I think she could help pull the sleigh tonight, if that's all right with you."

"What about Leah's present?" he asked. "It was meant to be very special."

"Don't worry," said Santa. "I will get your reindeer back to you as soon as I can. She will be well looked after. Rudolph, Head Reindeer, is a great chap and will help her all the way. I promise that Leah will have a reindeer this Christmas Day. Now, I need to change into my spare suit. I don't suppose there is any chance of a glass of sherry and a mince pie?"

Next morning, Leah woke and saw her bulging Christmas stocking. "It's Christmas!" she exclaimed, "and look! Santa has been."

On her bedside table was a beautifully carved wooden reindeer with a red bow around his neck and a card that read "LOVE, SANTA XXX".

The Check-Up

Every year the animals had a medical check-up to ensure that they were in good health.

"Cher Khan – your turn," said Dr Blister. "Teeth, fine. Coat, excellent condition. Eyes and ears, fine. Claws, fine. Weight, perfect. Everything all right for another year." Cher Khan jumped off the table and went out.

KoKo walked in and Dr Blister went through the same procedure with the same results. Then it was Tabby's turn.

"Now, Tabby. Teeth, fine. Coat, good. Eyes and ears, fine. Claws, could do with a bit of a trim. Weight – oh dear, oh dear. You are far too heavy to remain healthy. We must do something about it."

"But I'm OK," said Tabby. "Perfectly happy. No problems."

"No problems at the moment," said the vet, "but you are storing them up for the future. The weight is putting an extra strain on your heart, and on your bones. Carry on like you're doing and you could even develop a nasty illness called diabetes which would mean you would have to stay on a special diet for the rest of your life, and medication, too."

Tabby hung his head and started to cry. "But I love eating," he moaned.

"Everything in moderation," said Dr Blister. "Dieting can be fun – especially with exercise. You could start by climbing a few trees."

"I haven't climbed a tree in years," said Tabby, tears rolling off his whiskers.

"Then time to start. Nothing like the present!" Dr Blister replied briskly. "Here's a diet sheet with pictures. Three sensible meals a day, and no snacking!"

Tabby glanced at it. "No spider pies!" he exclaimed miserably.

"That's right," said the vet, "but spiders are all right on their own... ah, how about spider soup? Or, maybe spider omelette. Both are delicious."

Tabby regarded him miserably.

"Now, the next thing is exercise, but you can start in a small way. Let's say, climb three trees a day. Also, Lady Margo, from Little Chirp Manor, runs an Animal Fitness Class once a week."

"Oh my goodness! No... oh. She makes everyone run like soldiers!" Tabby said, terrified.

"But she is an excellent coach. Now, I'll book you on the next class. No excuses. Come back next month and we'll review your progress."

Lady Margo had a very grand house. She loved giving dinner parties, but worked off all the excellent food with plenty of keep-fit exercises and running.

"Gather around, everyone," she said to the class. "Welcome to our new arrival, Tabby.

Now, we'll start with a gentle warm-up. Ten laps around the tennis court. First one in gets a spider. One, two, three, go!"

The class trotted off.

"Wow!" Tabby said to himself, puffing and panting. Sweat dripped down his face and he finished last.

"No spider today,." said Lady Margo, "but this is your first of many classes, so we have our high hopes."

Tabby groaned. He was totally worn out and went back home for a long sleep.

Over the next few weeks Tabby found the classes getting easier, and his diet sheet helped his owner to give him tasty meals which made him feel full. All too soon it was time for his review with Dr Blister.

"Excellent progress!" said the vet. "You must be feeling a lot healthier, too."

"Yes," replied Tabby.. "I won't get stuck in a window again!"

Caramel Eyes, the caretaker, was sprucing up her long, luxuriant coat as he prepared to leave. She eyed him curiously.

"You look completely different now, Tabby," she said. "A fine figure of a cat."

Tabby preened himself and looked smug.

"Have you ever considered getting married?" she enquired.

"No, no, never. Not for me," he replied, embarrassed.

"But look at Raj and Taj, the tigers. They're really happy together. Maybe we could make a go of it. What do you say?" She batted her eyelashes at him.

For the first time Tabby really appreciated all the running that Lady Margo had made him do, and he was out through the door in a flash.

Acknowledgements

To my very dear and much loved friend, Jim Anthony, who has helped make this book possible.

The wonderful Maggie Attfield, whose illustrations bought the animals to life.

My sisters, Marguerite Wilson and Nanci Lister, who provided inspiration and criticism.

Jamie and Leah Mills, who helped with technical and practical support.

Lastly, I dedicate this book to my father, Edward Colston Stewart. A former squadron leader with Bomber Command in WW11. A master storyteller.